COLOR TEST PAGE

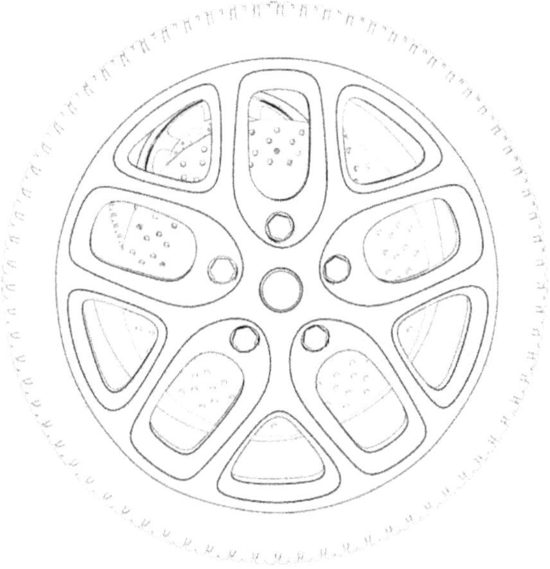
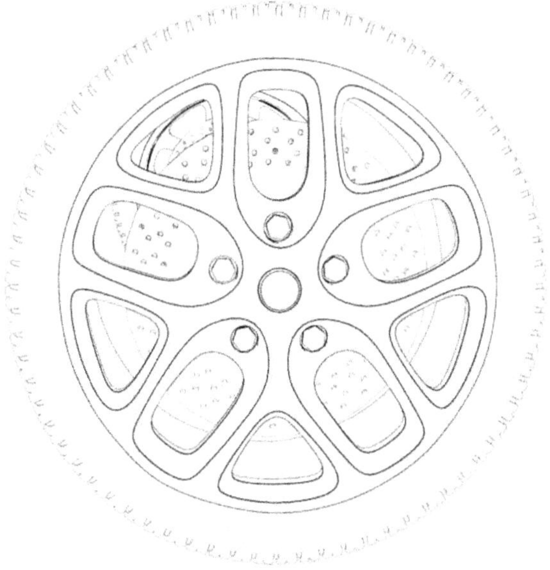
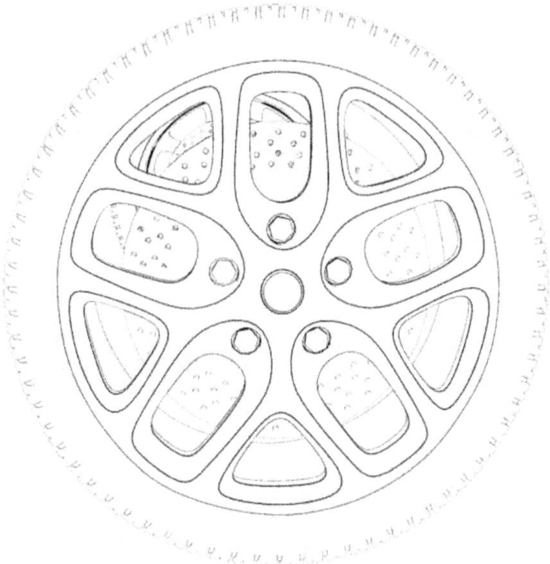
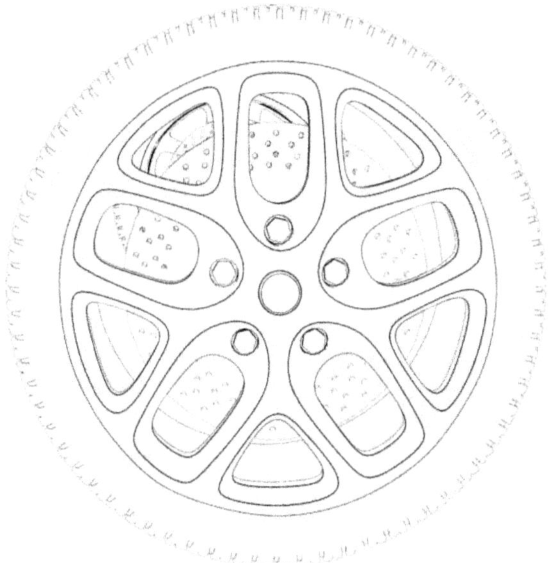
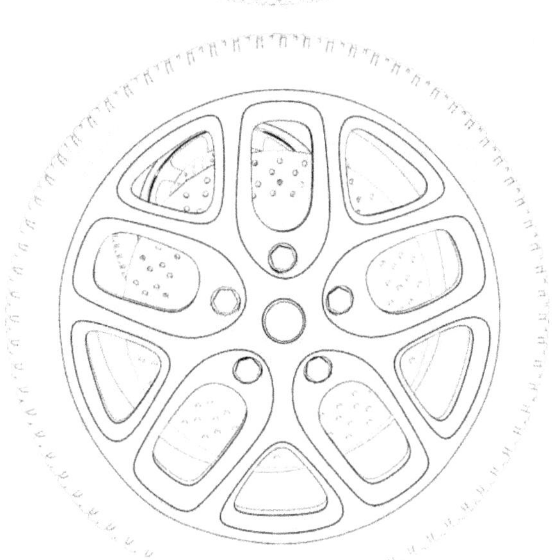
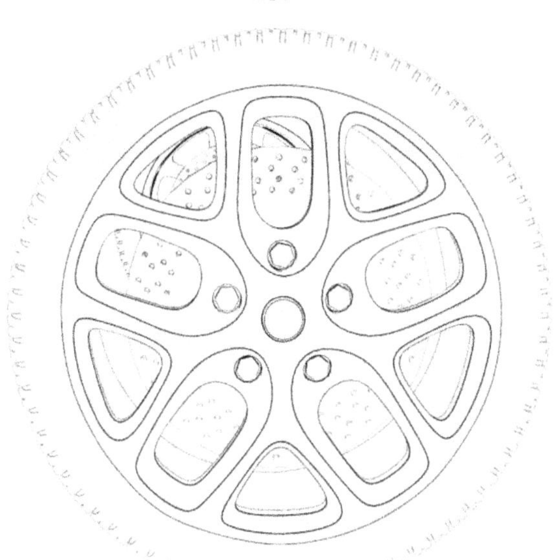

COLOR TEST PAGE

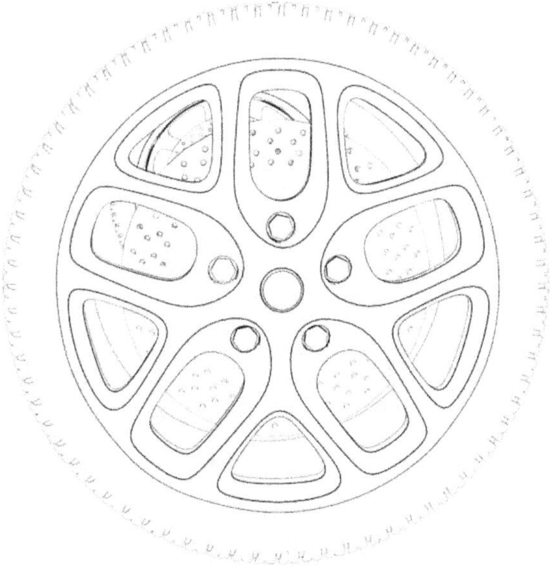
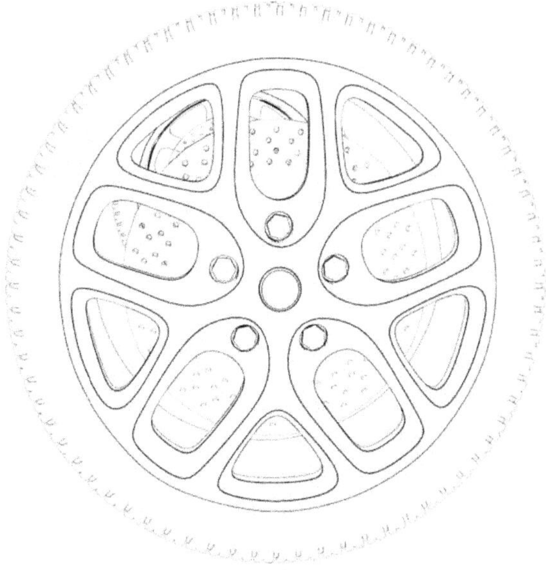
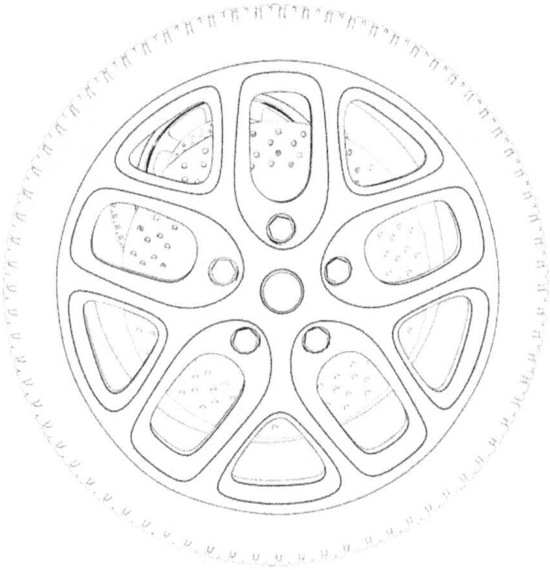
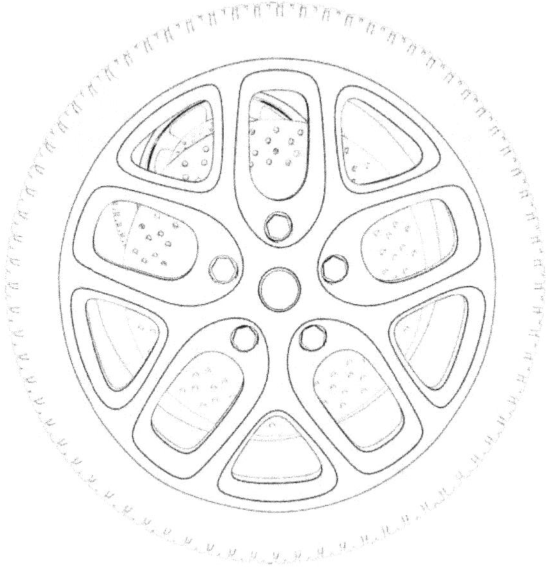
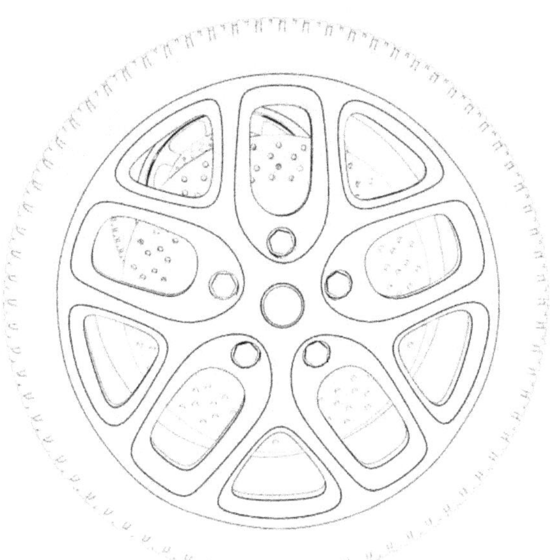
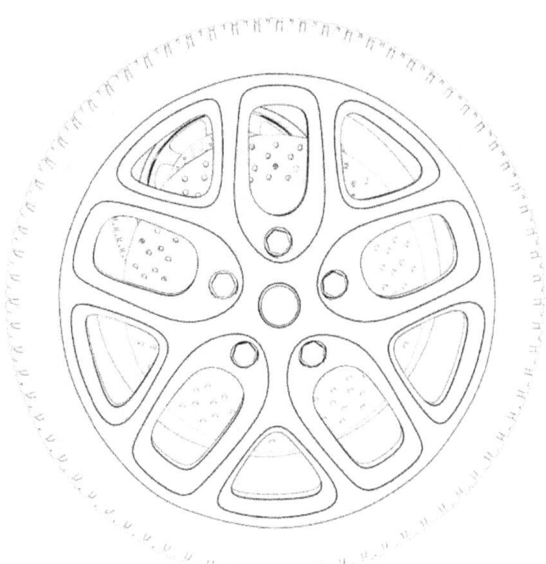

COLOR TEST PAGE

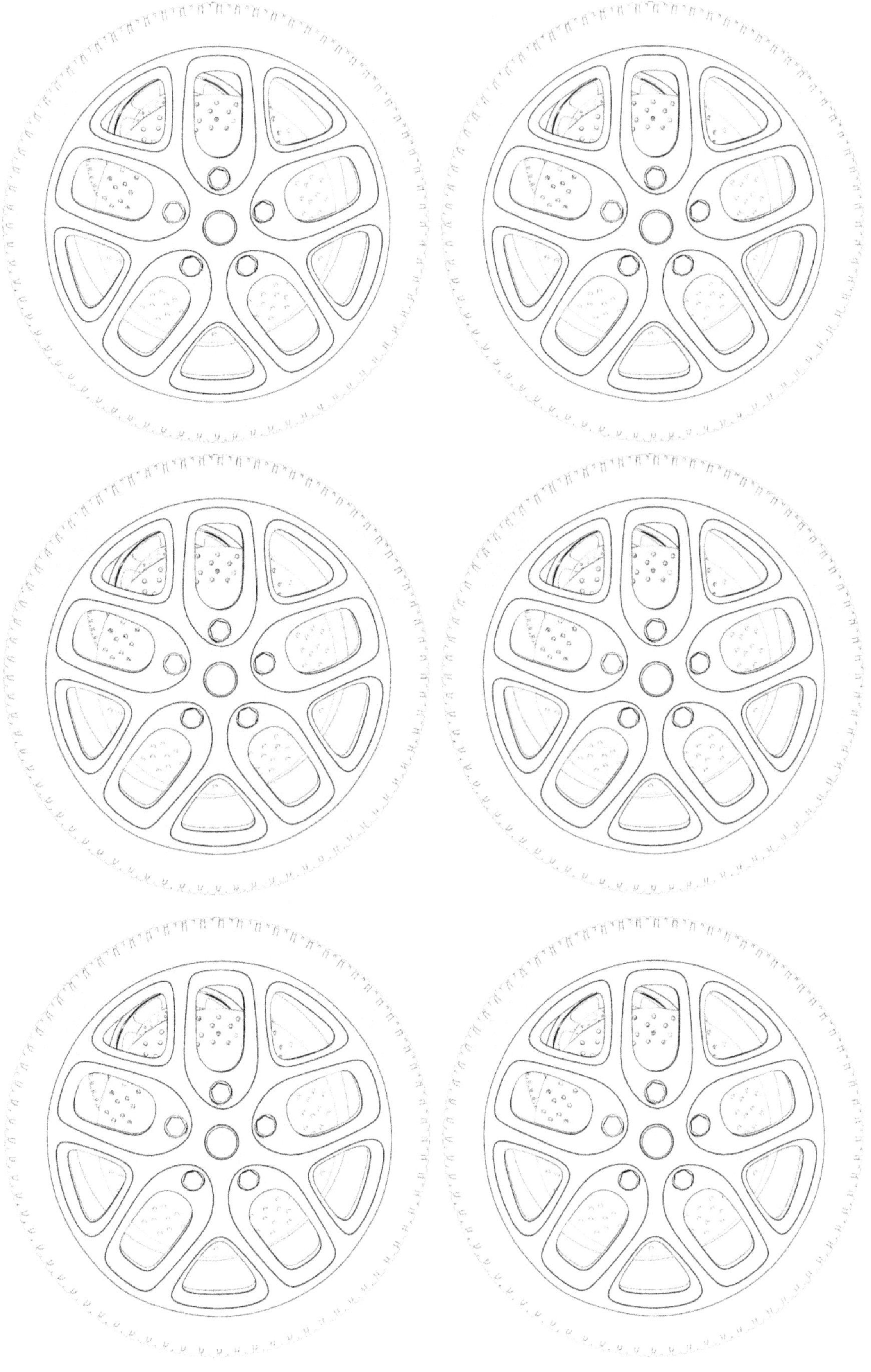

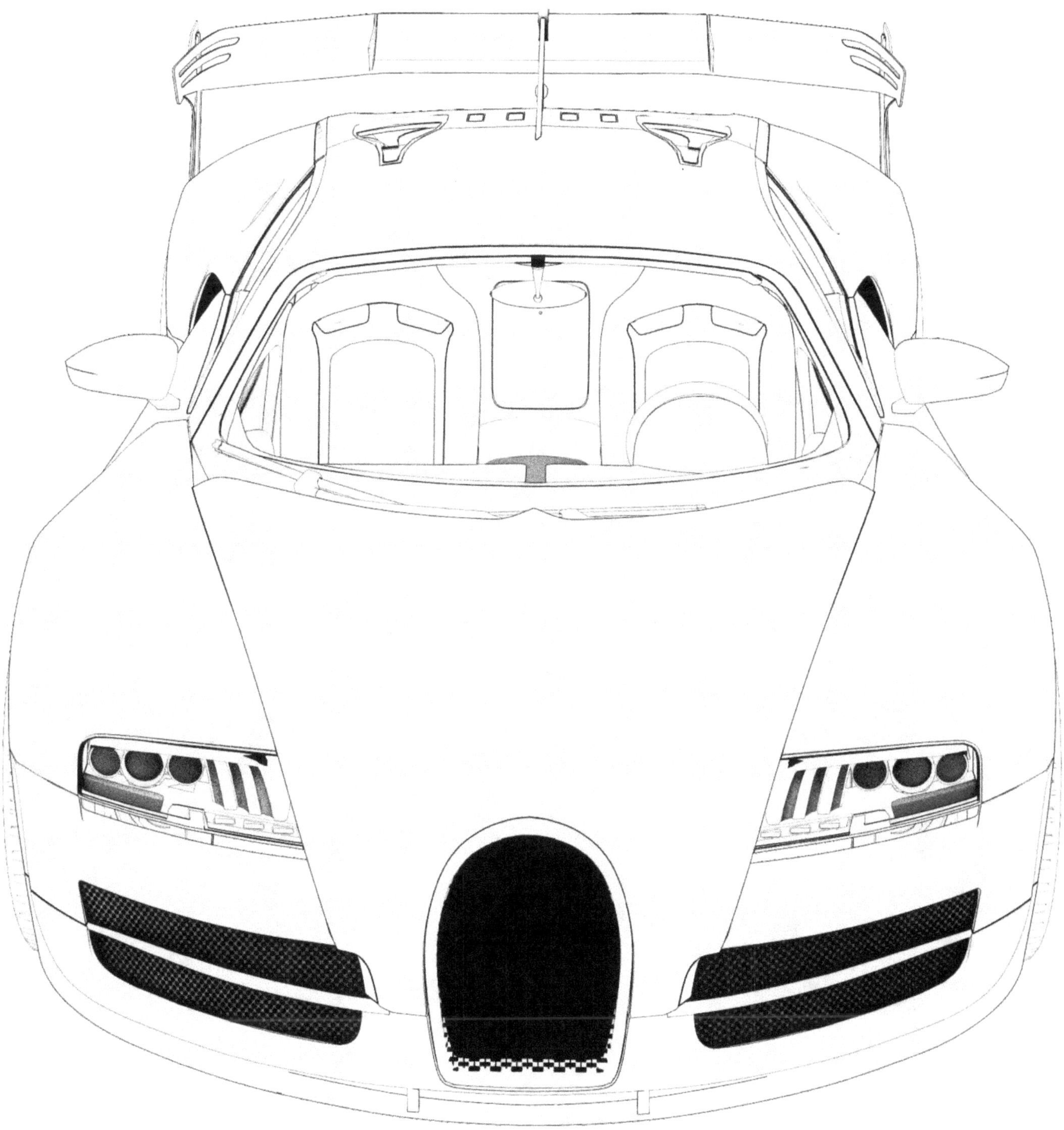

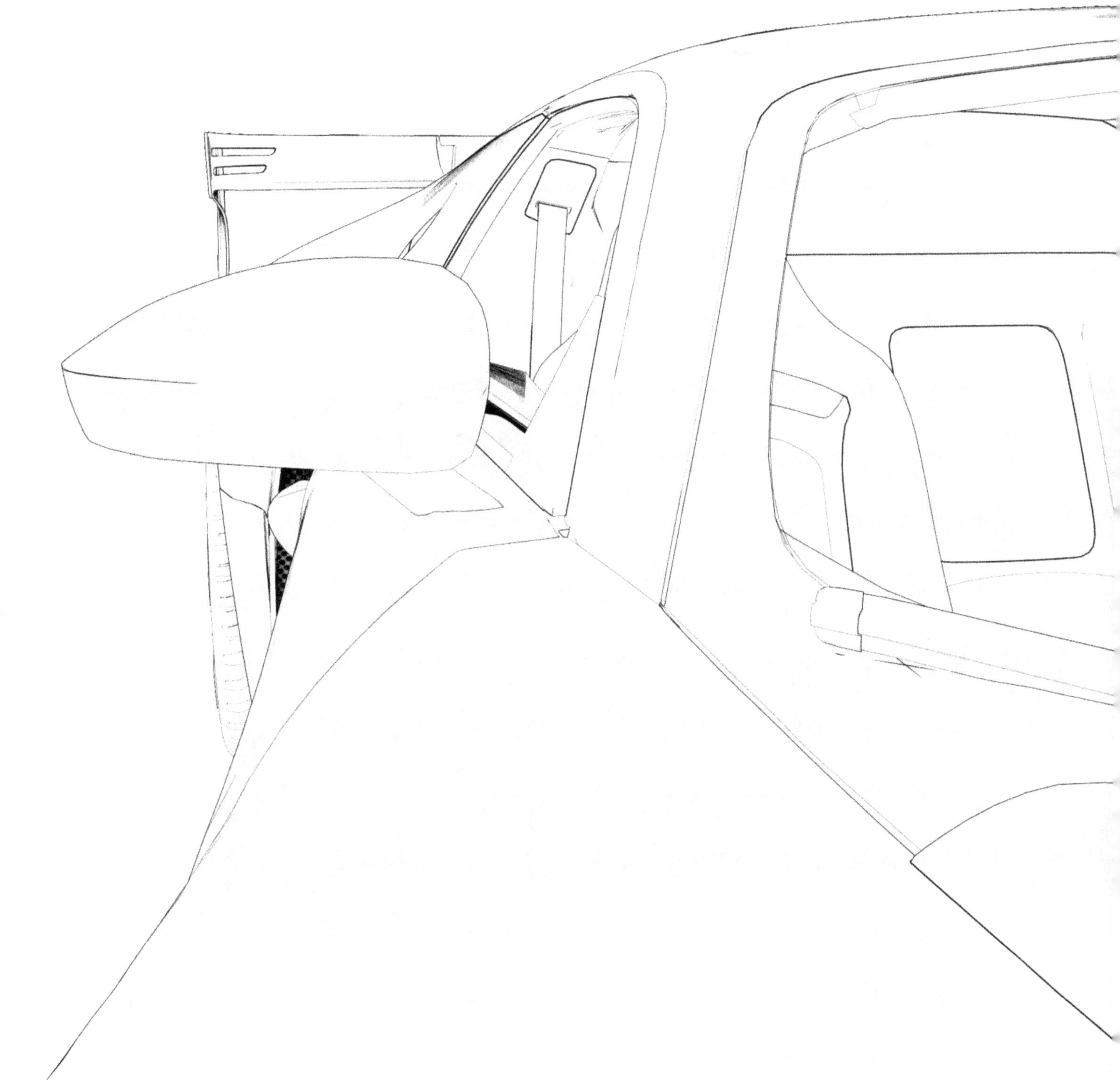

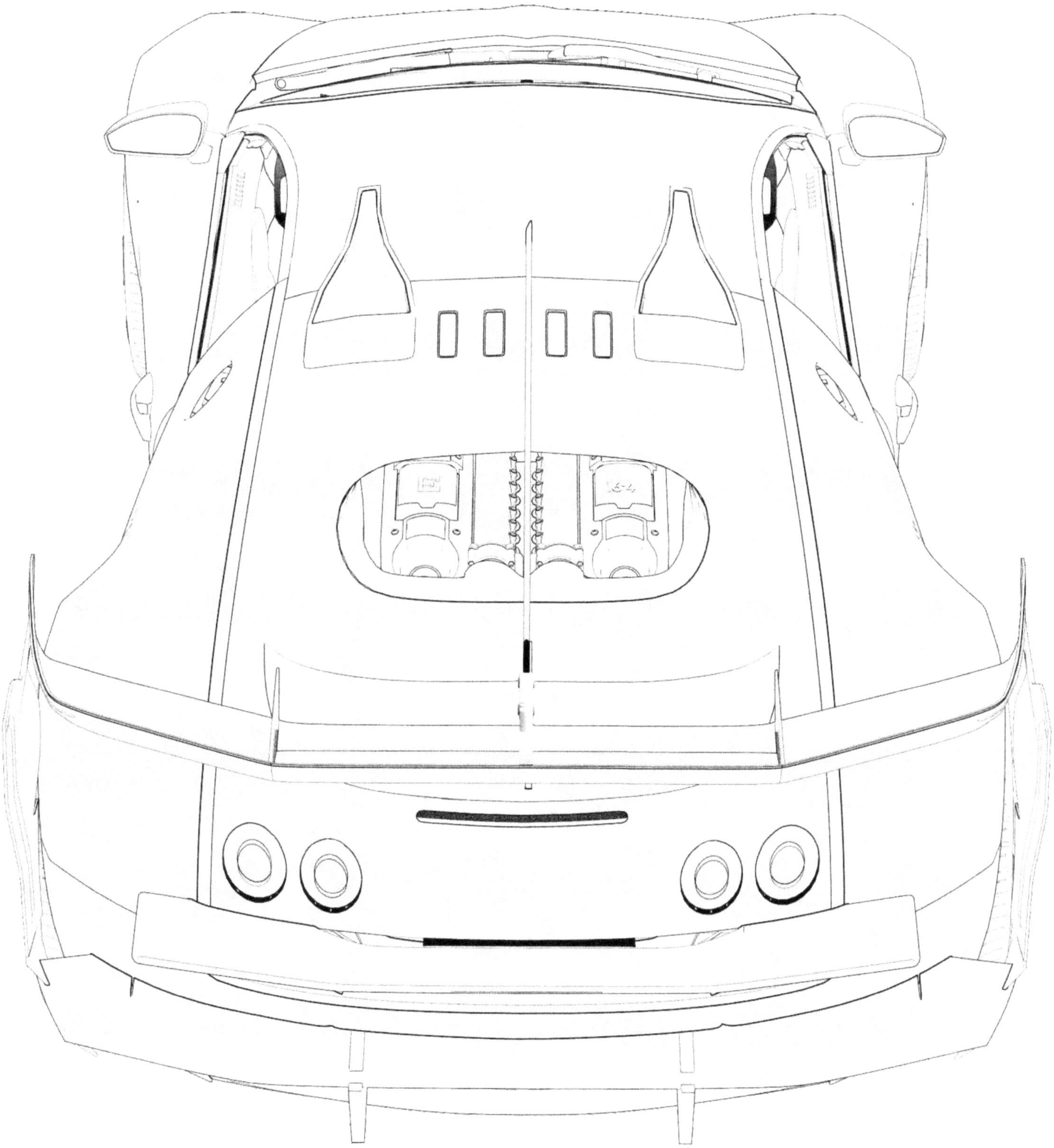

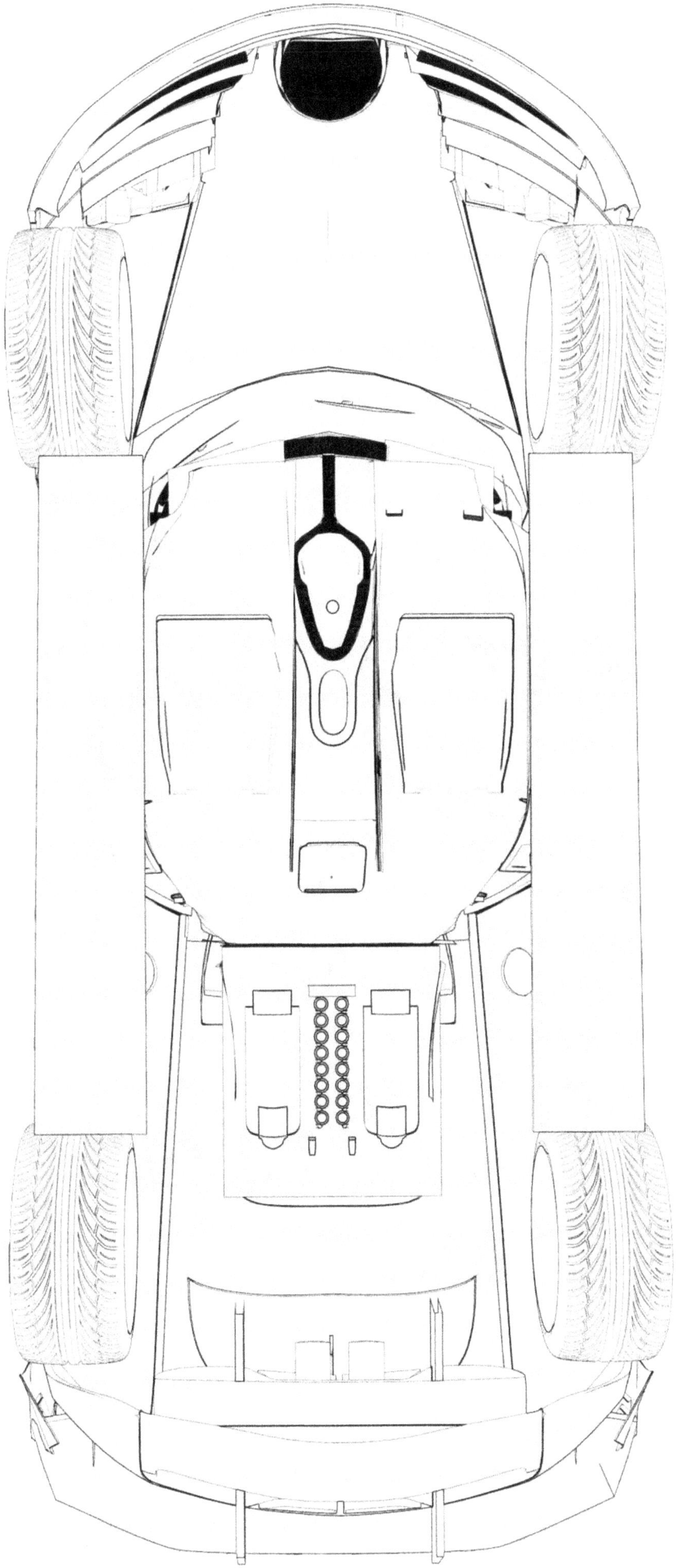

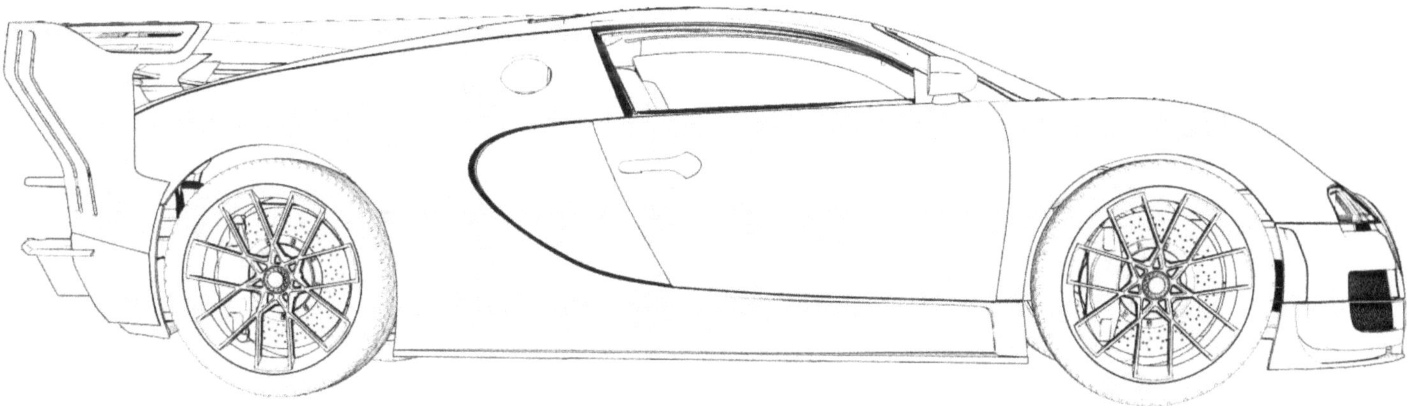

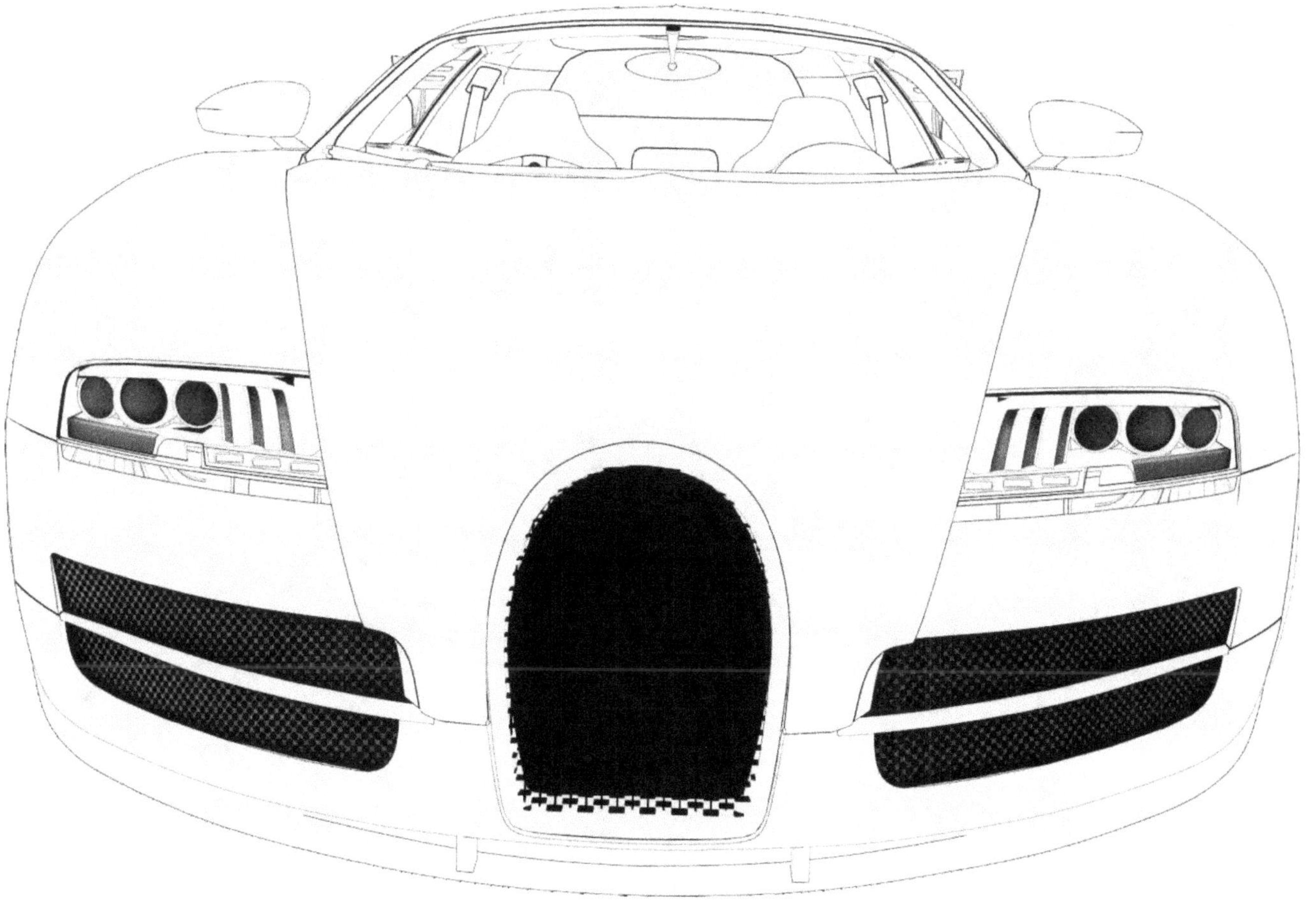

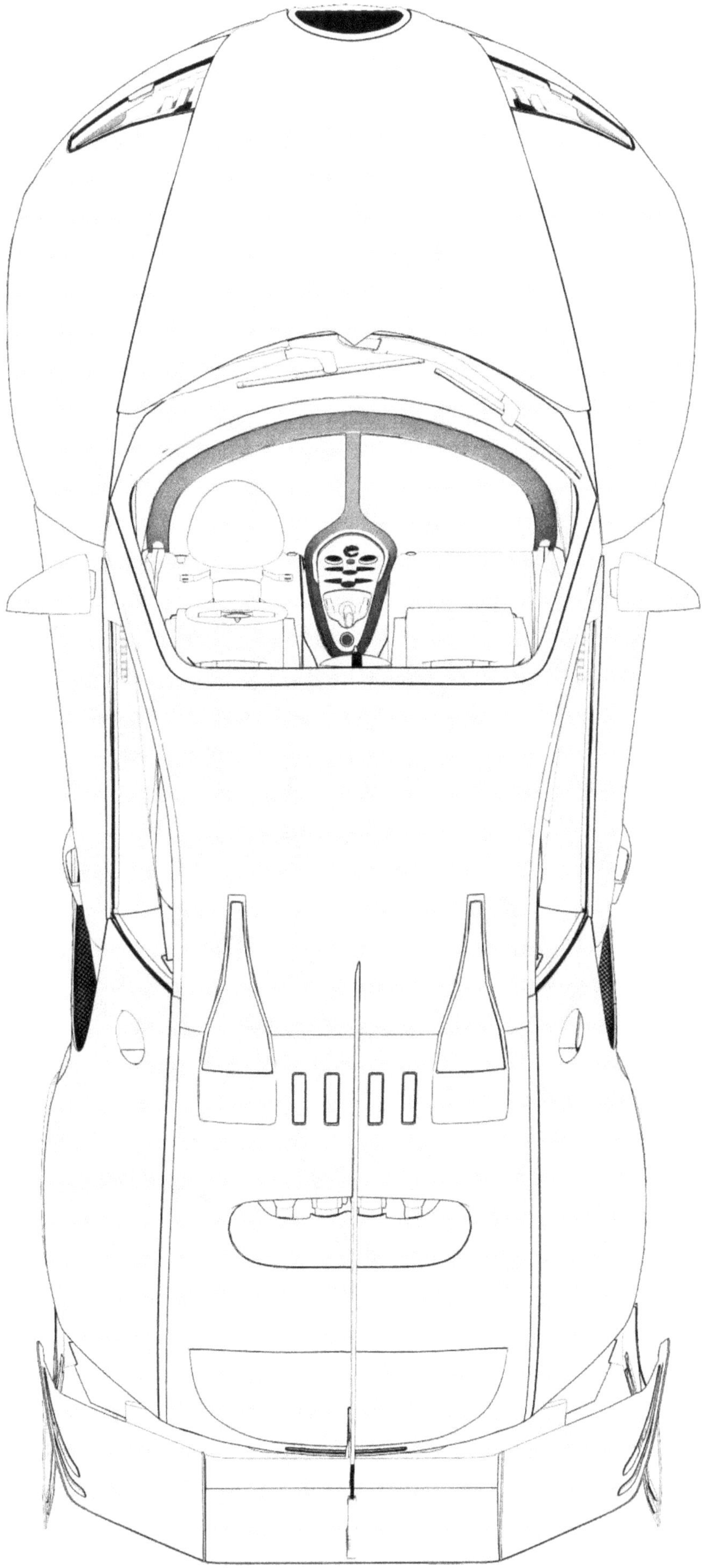

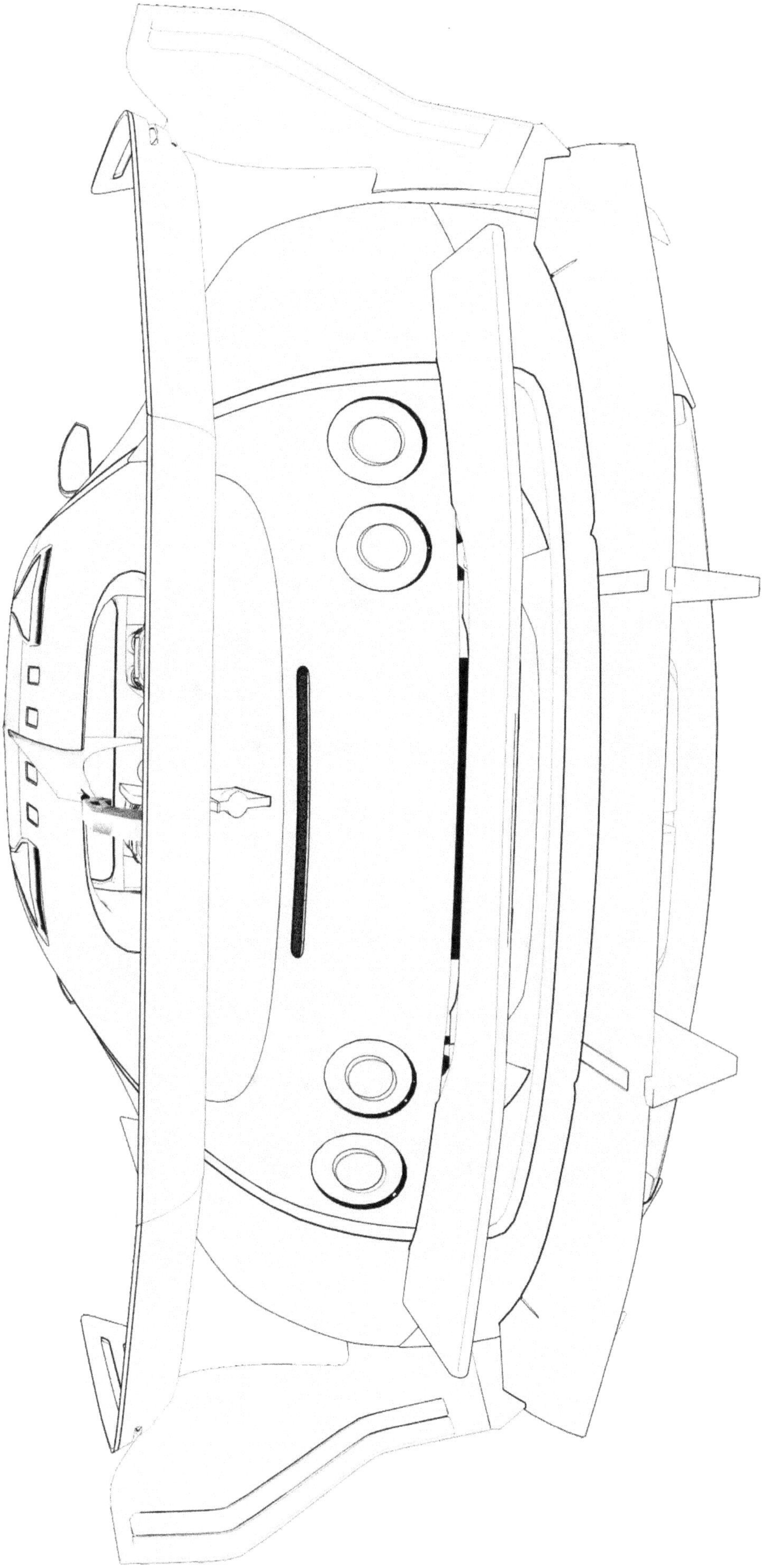

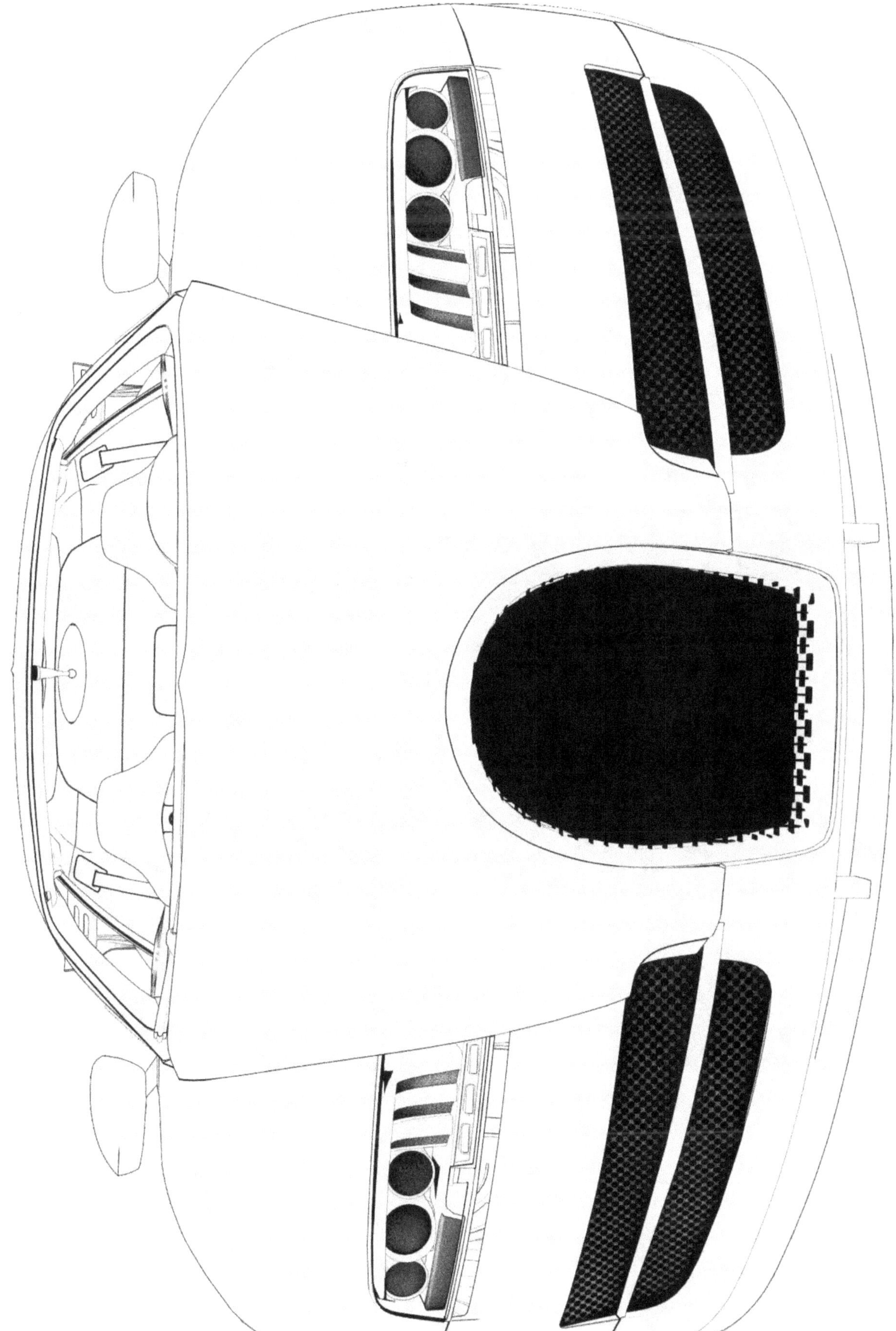

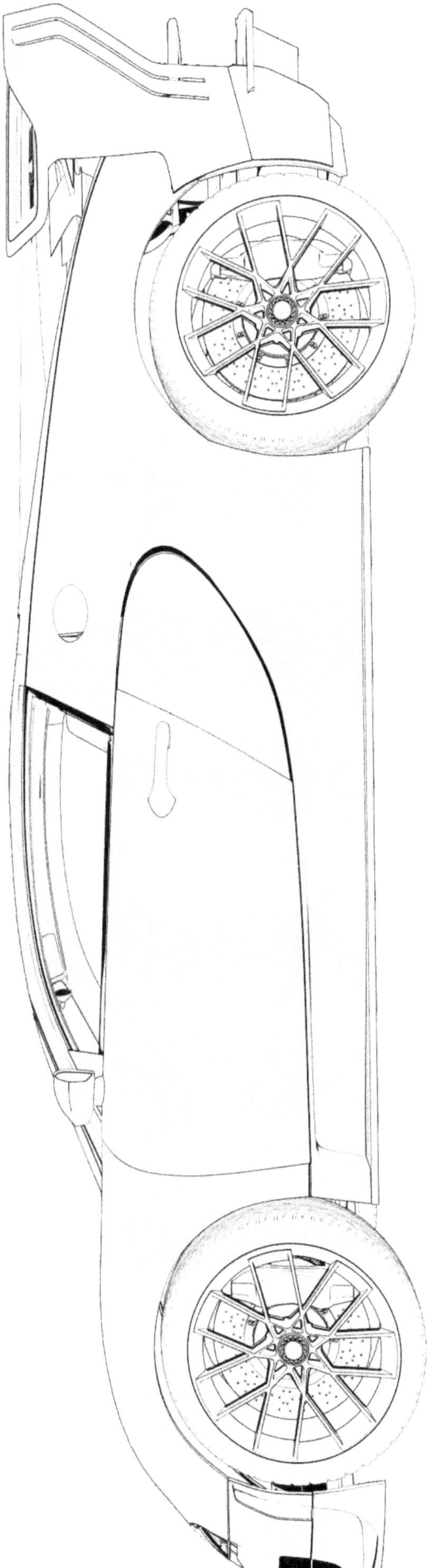

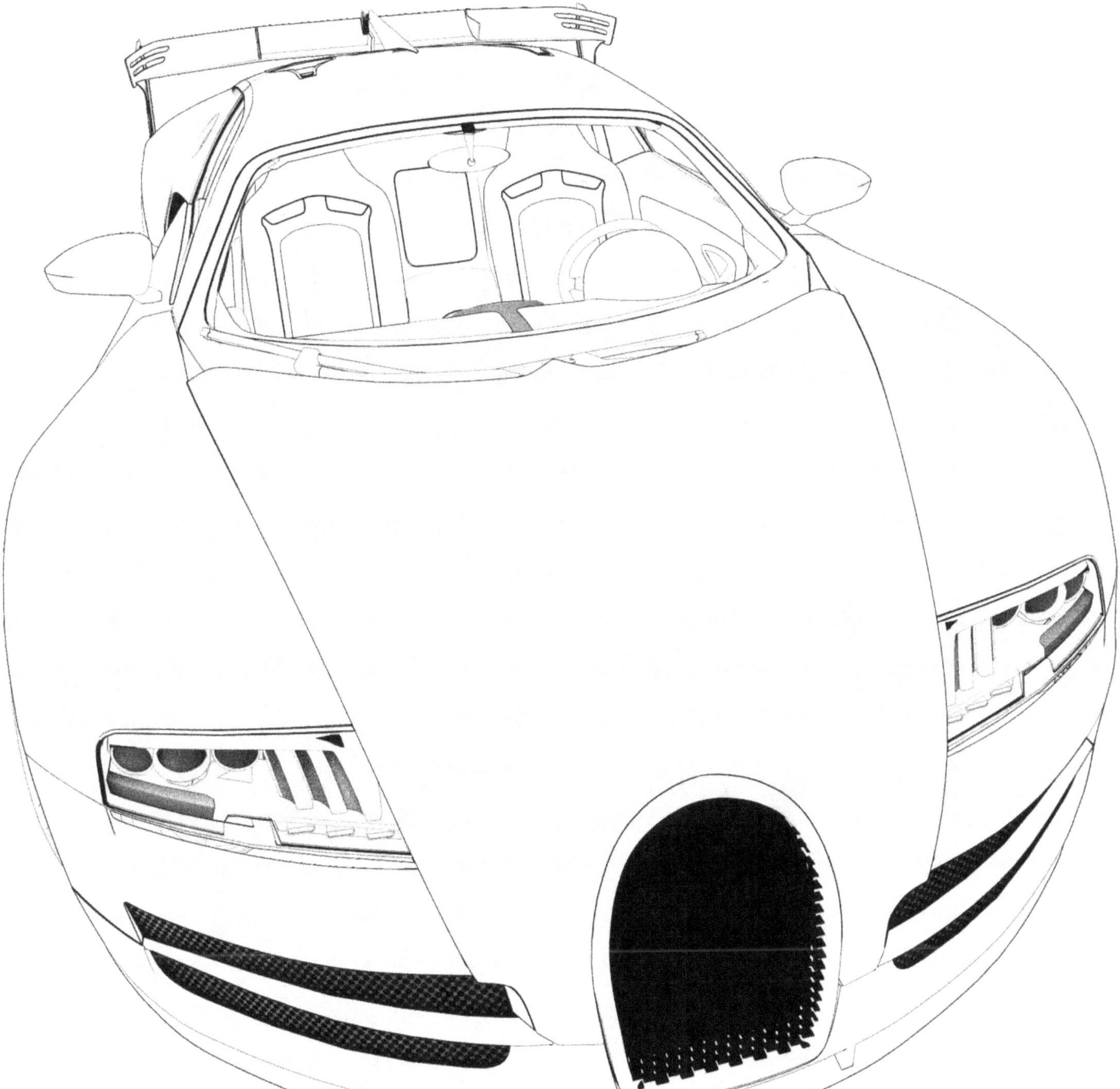

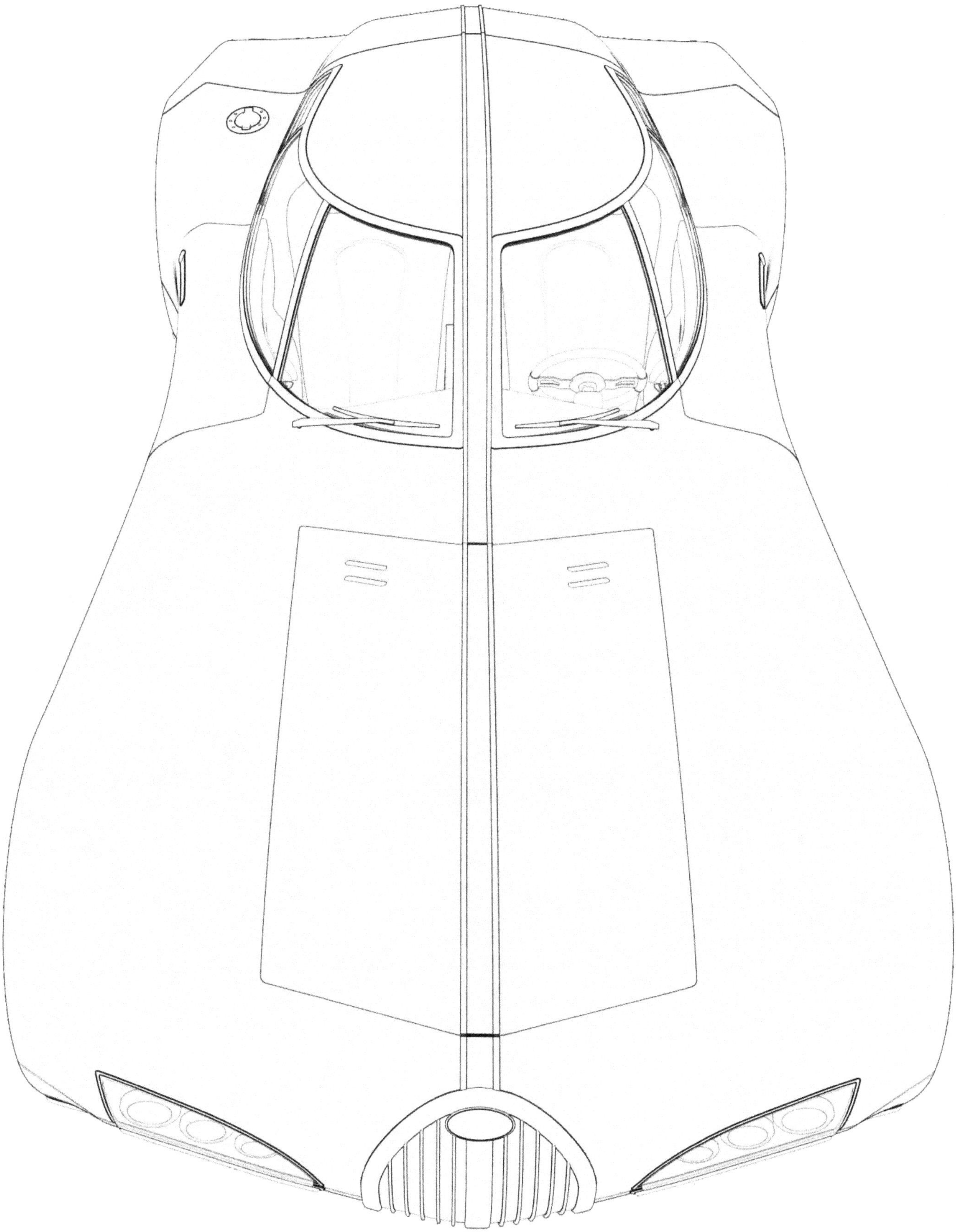

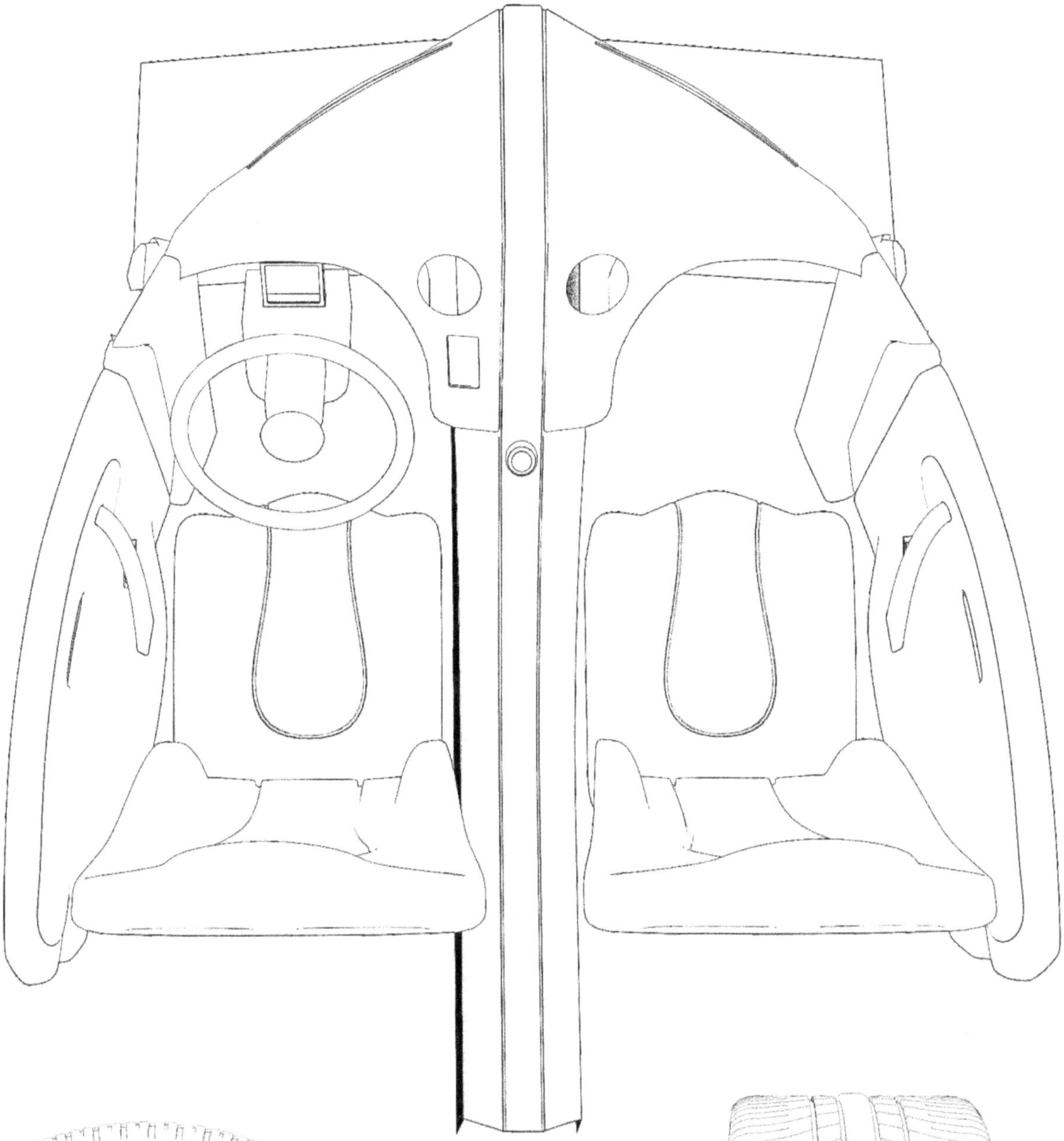

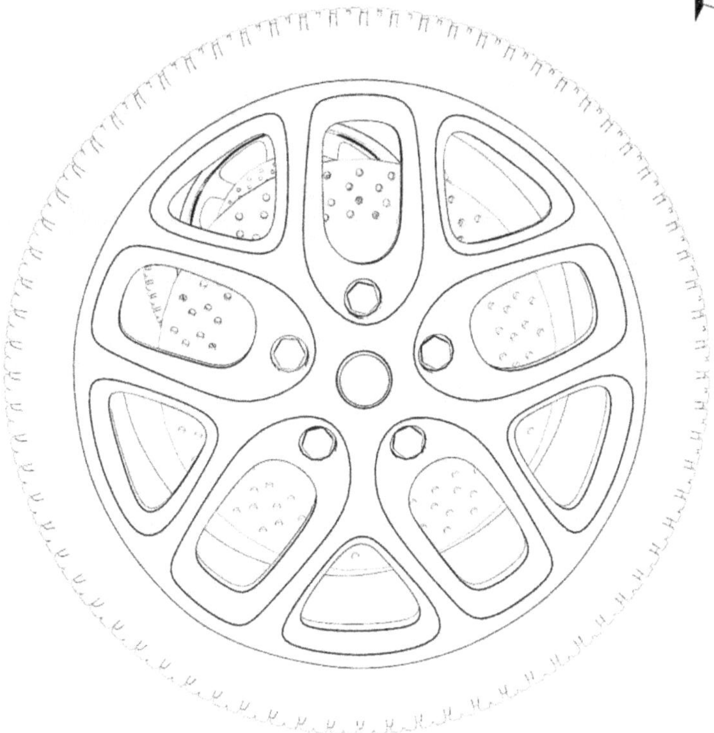

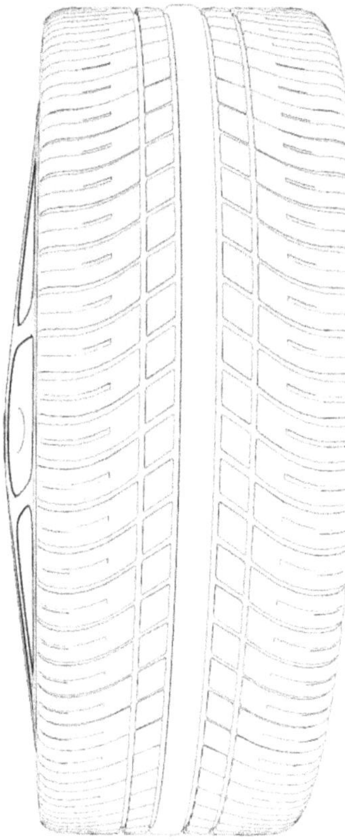

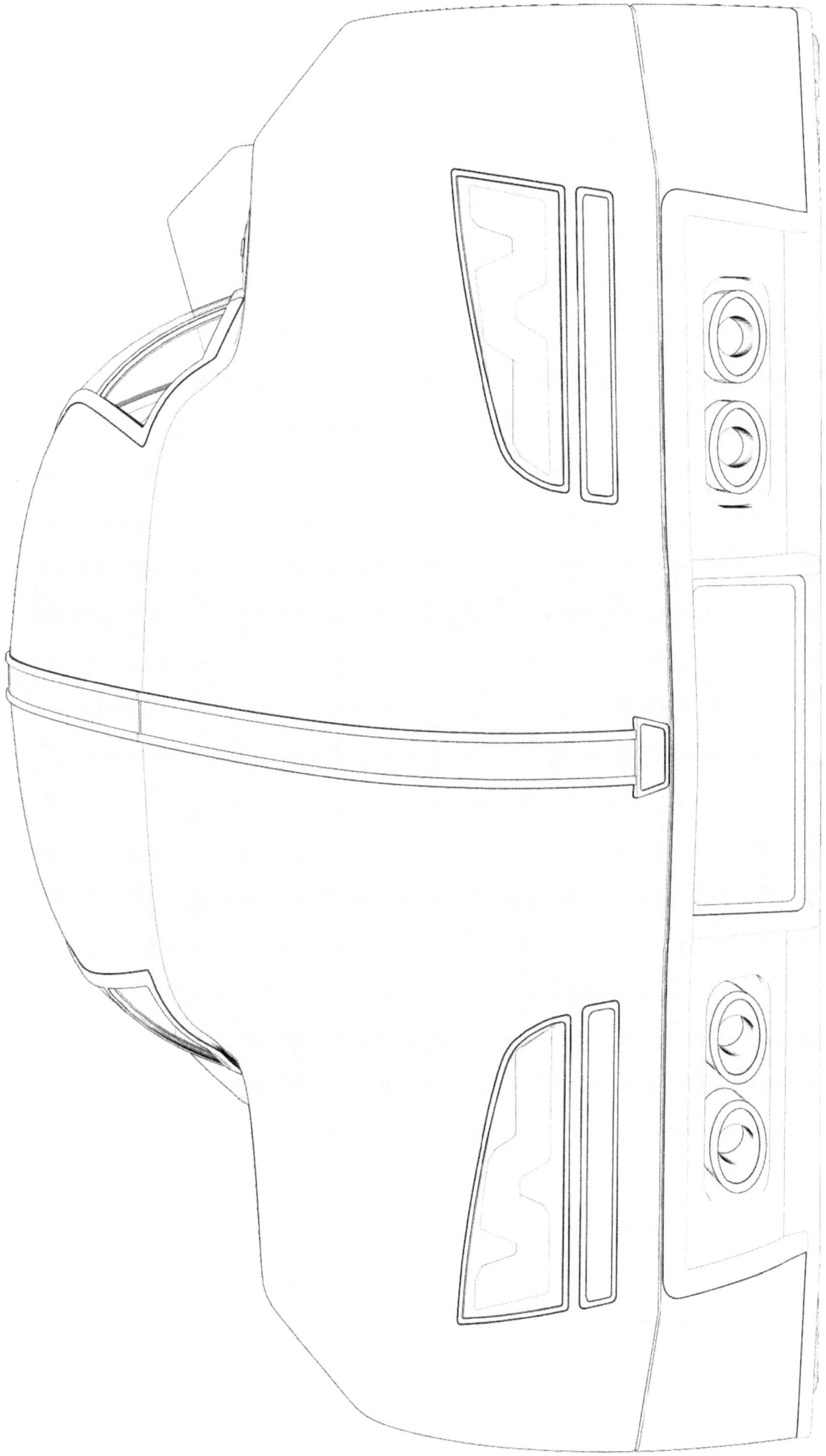

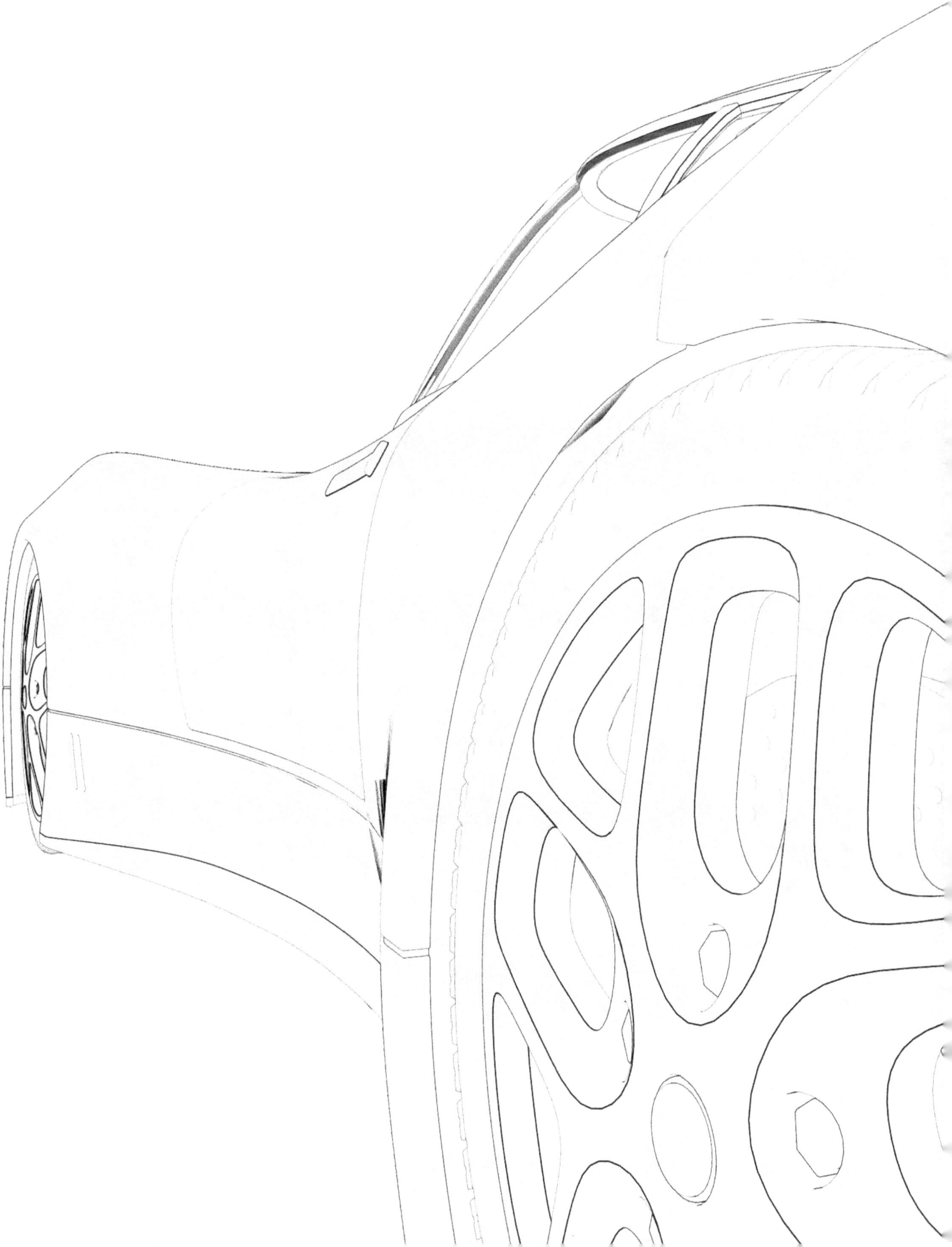

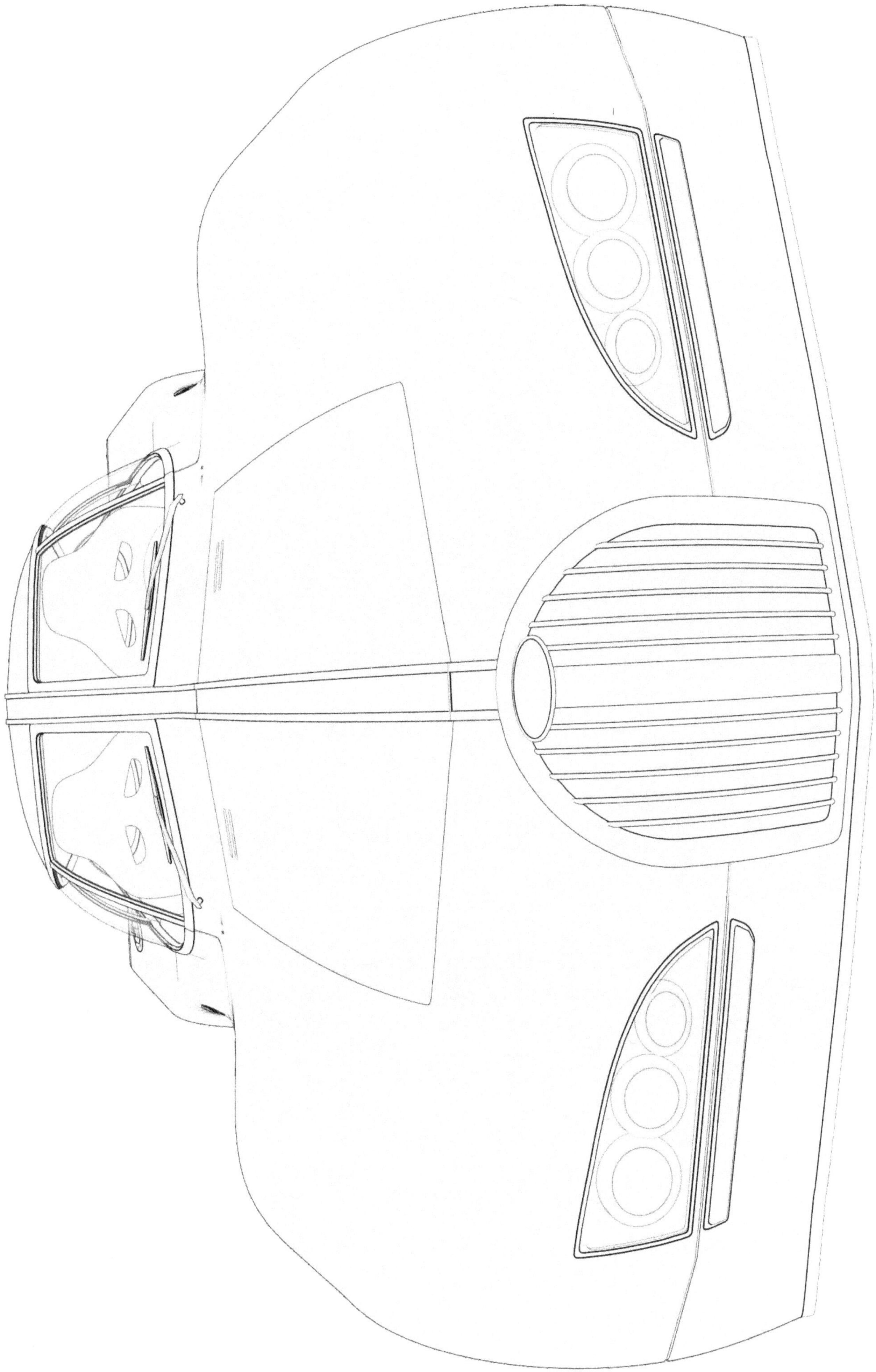

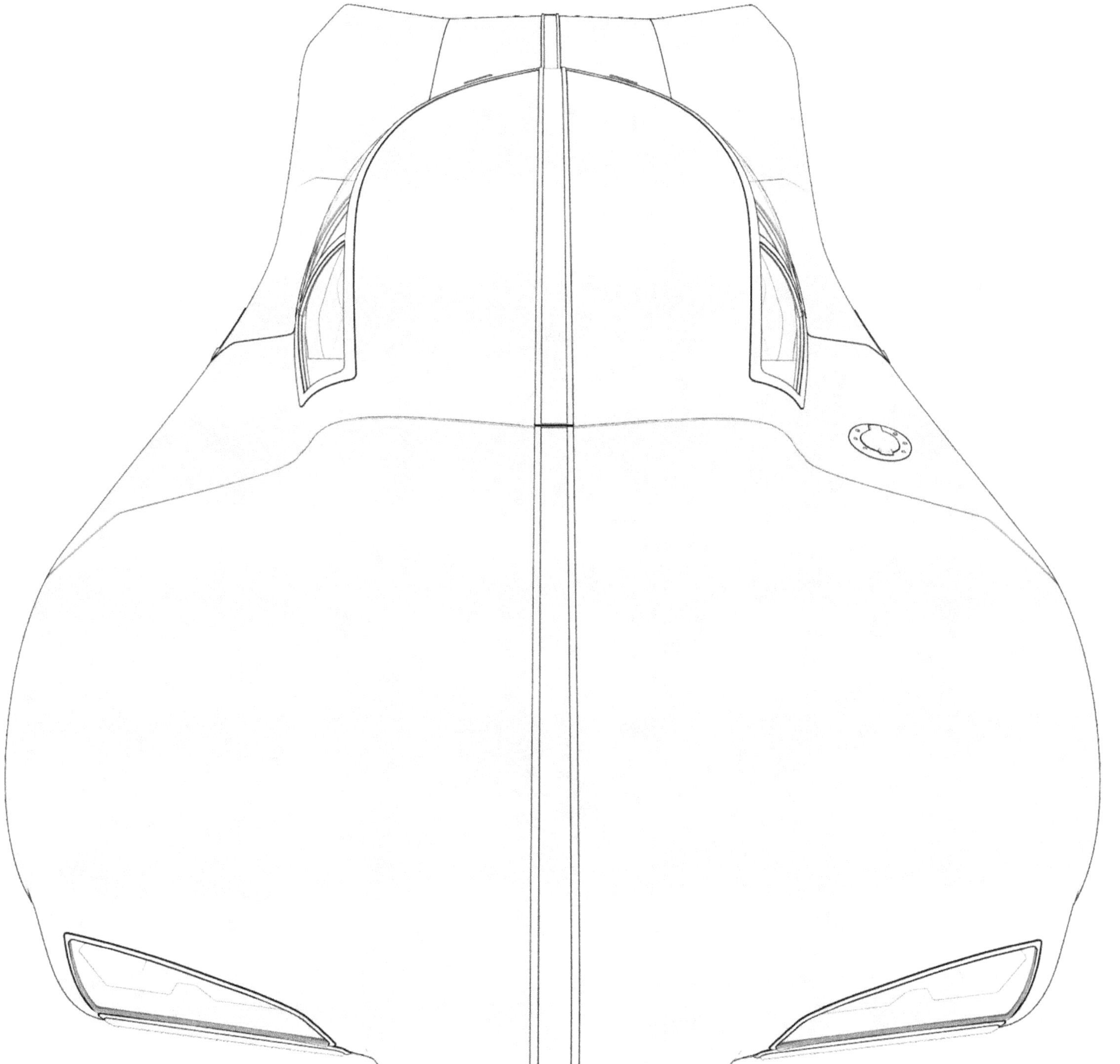

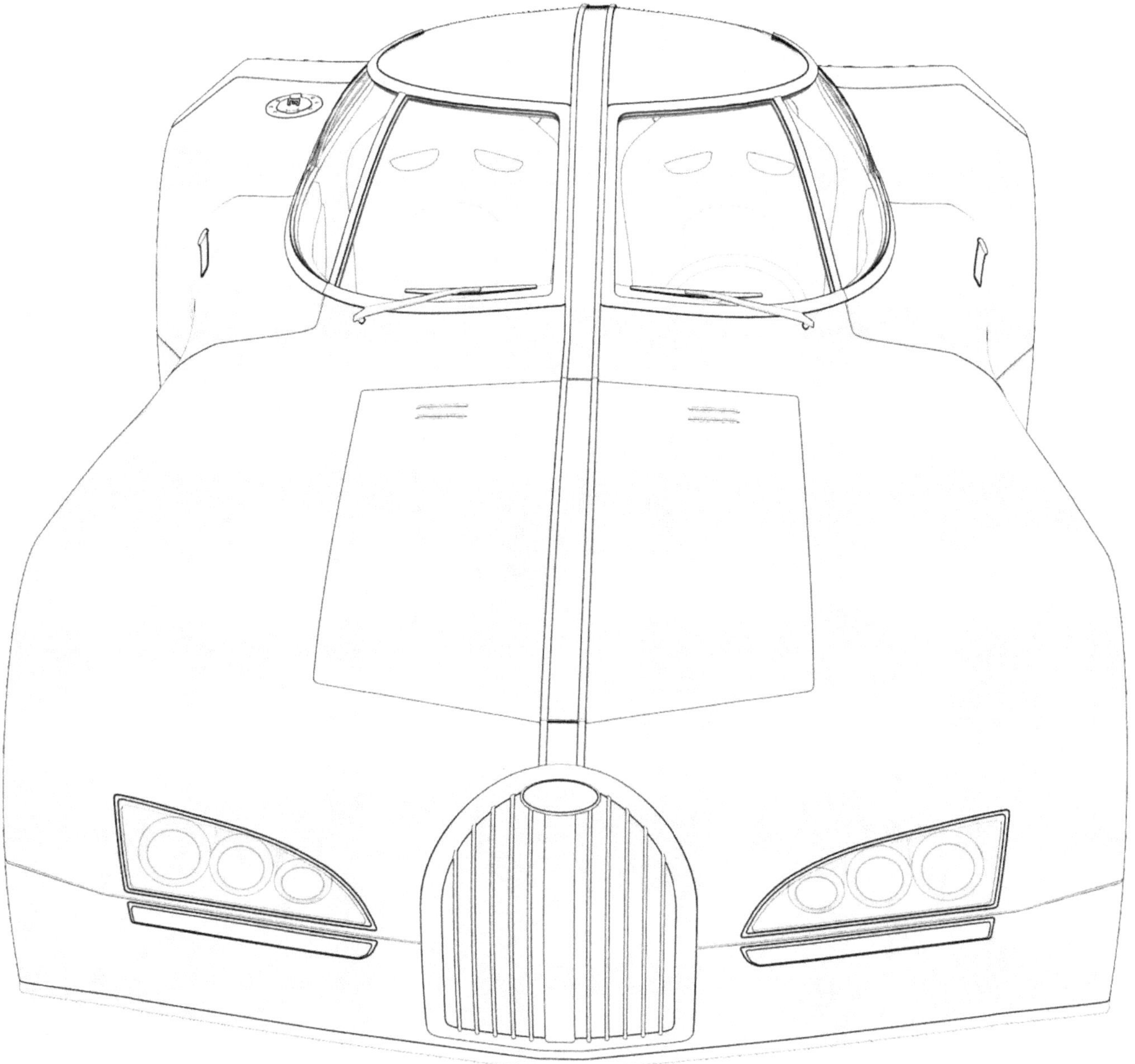

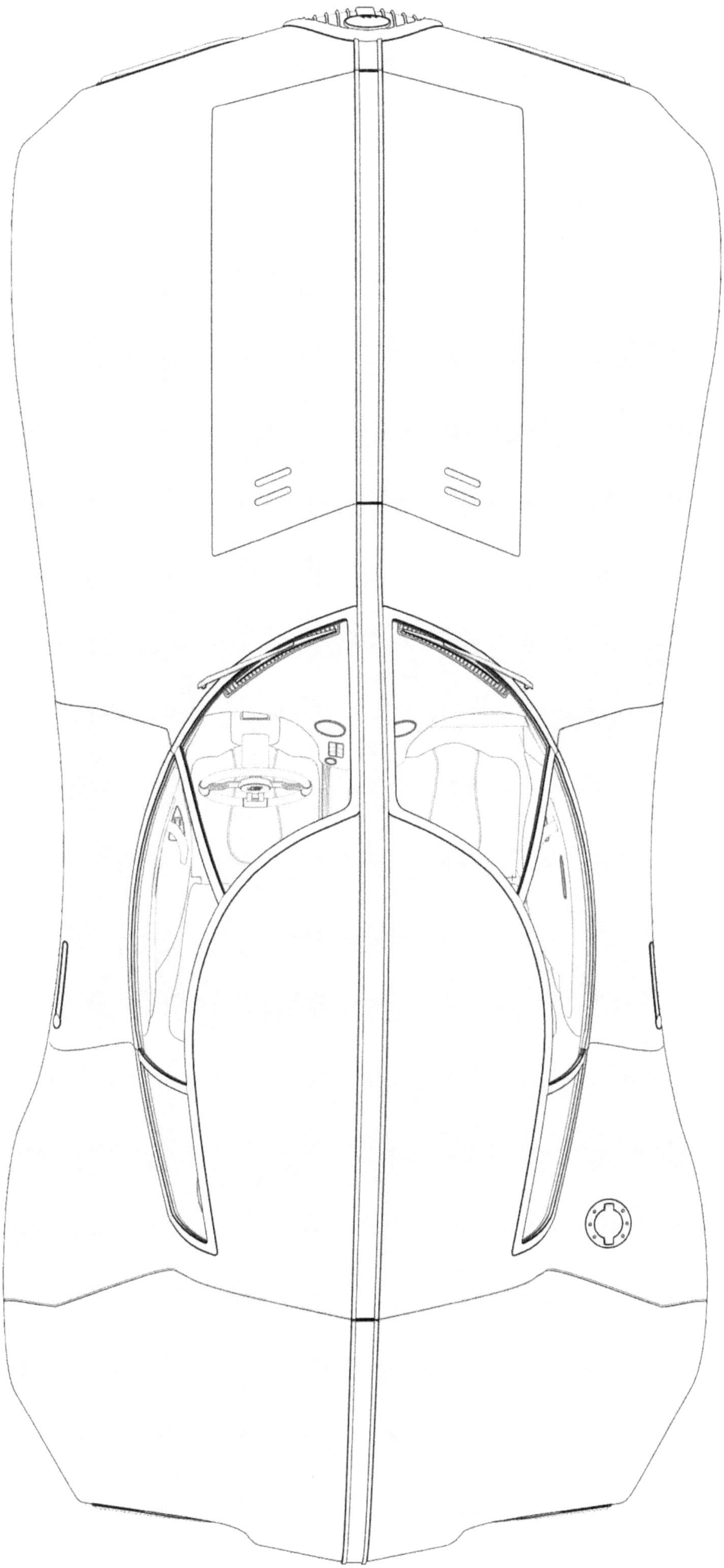

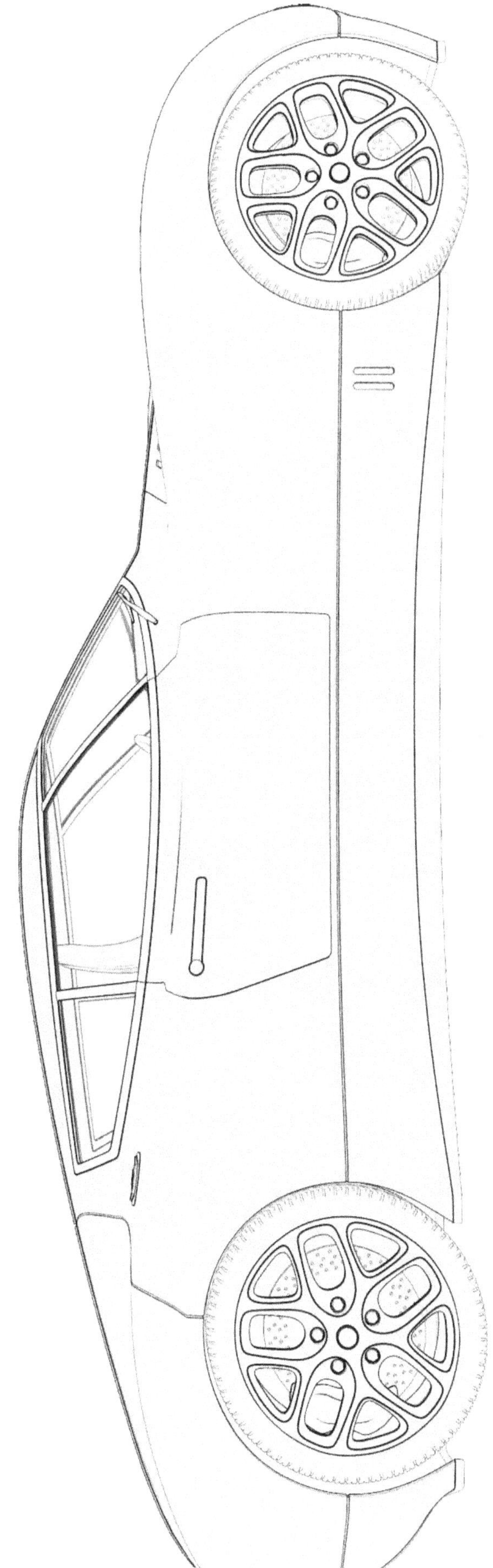

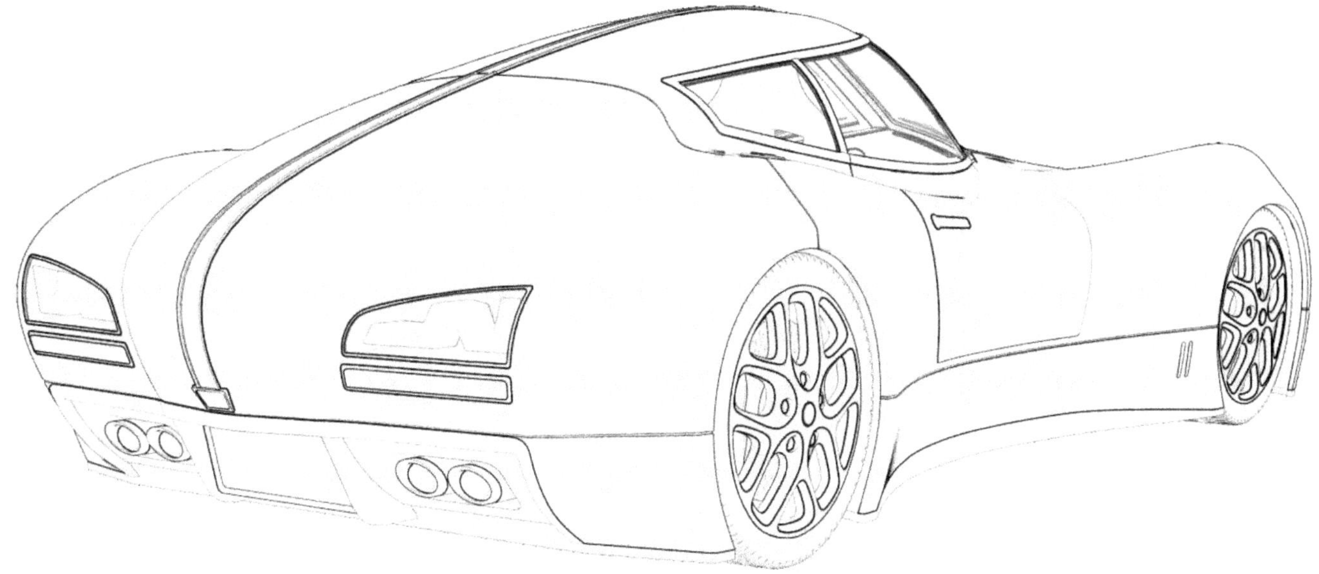

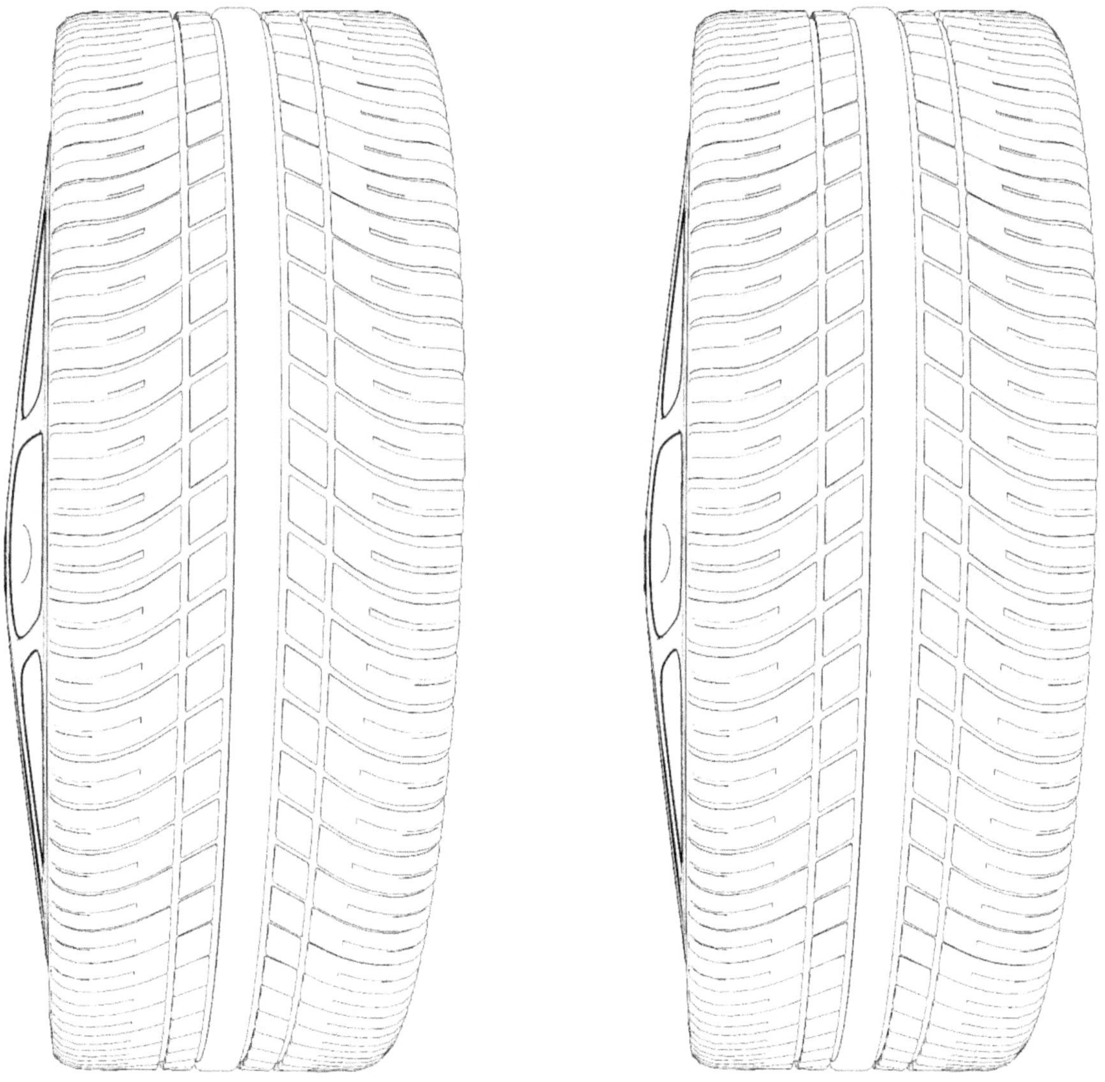

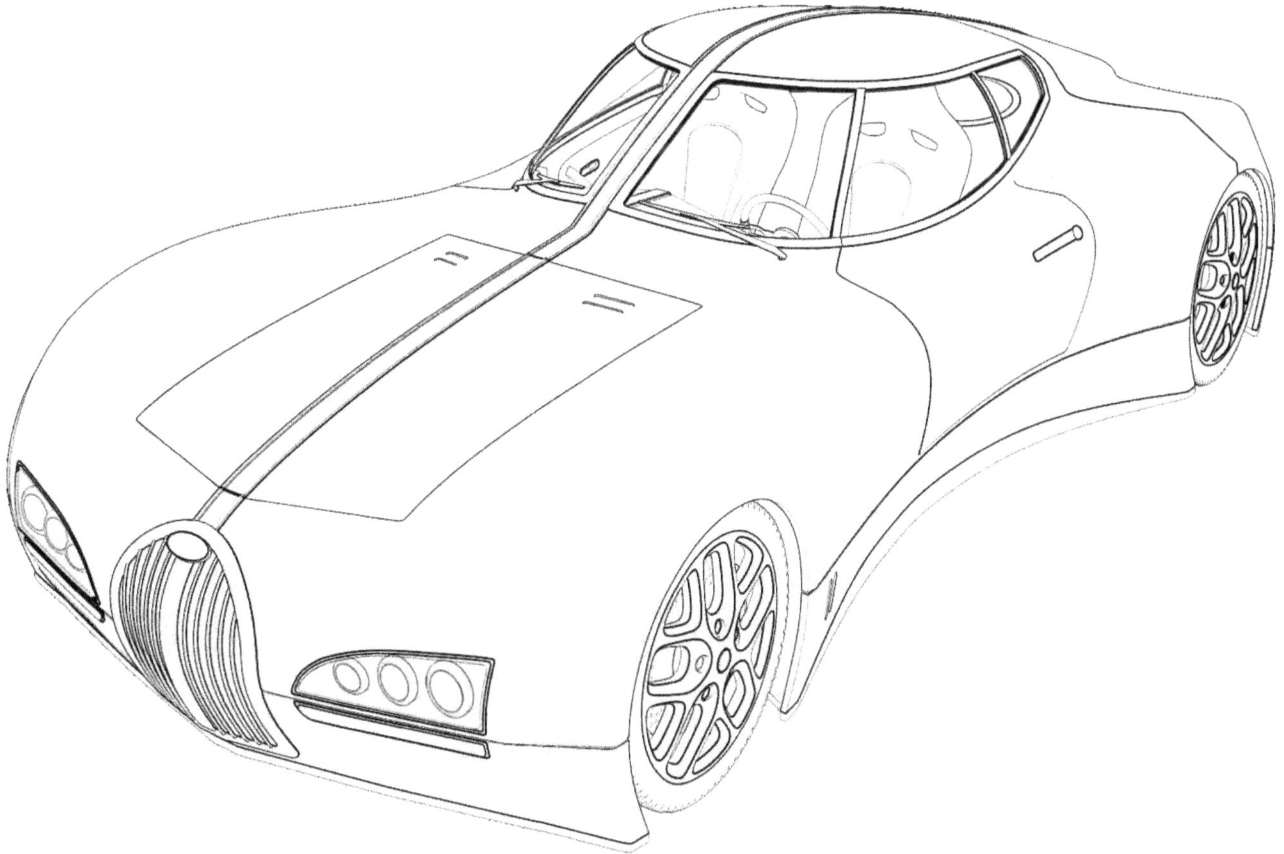
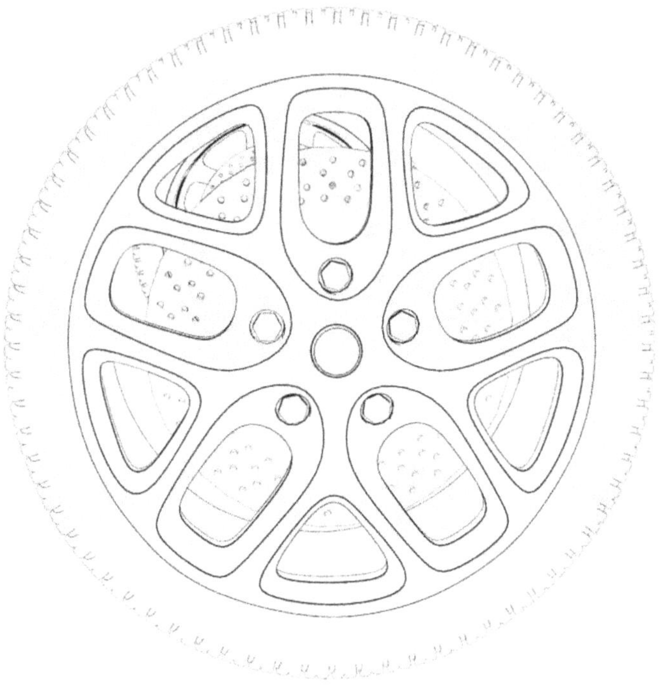
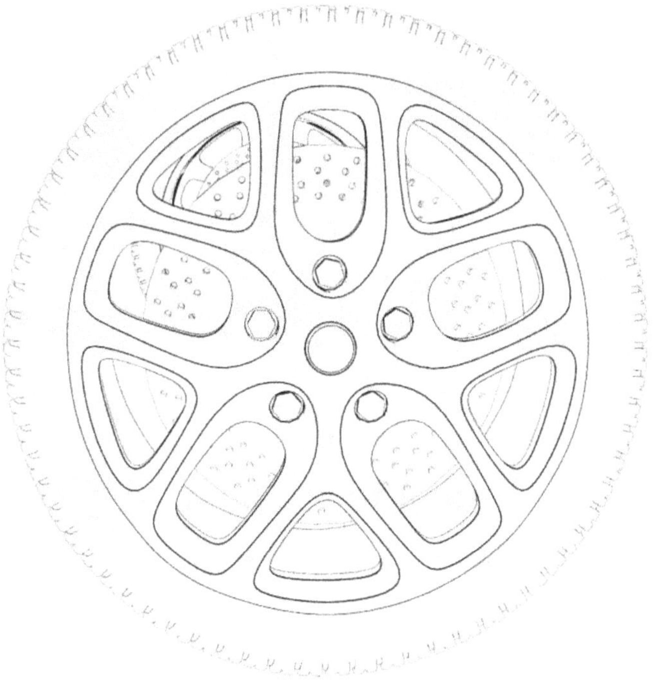

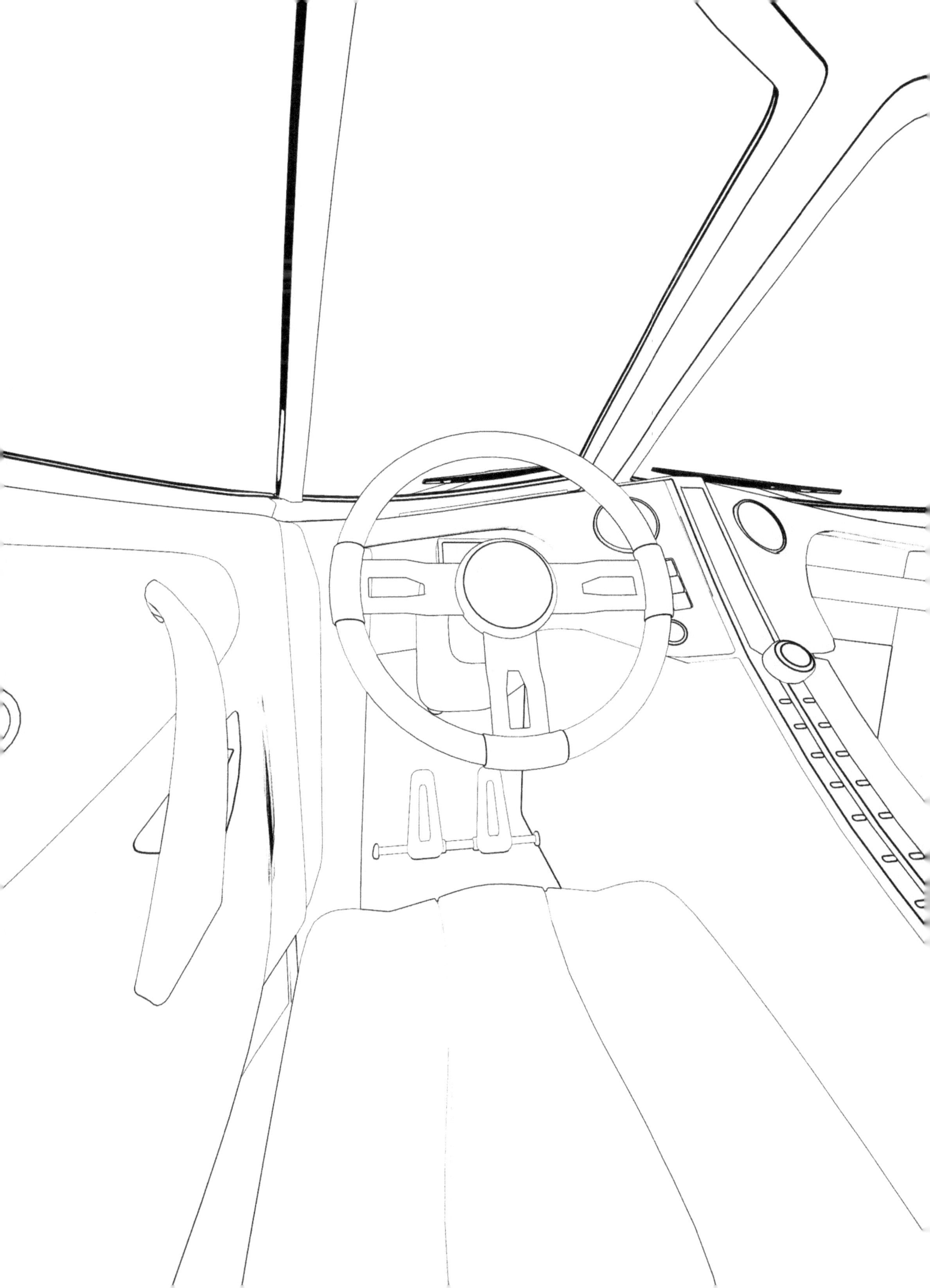

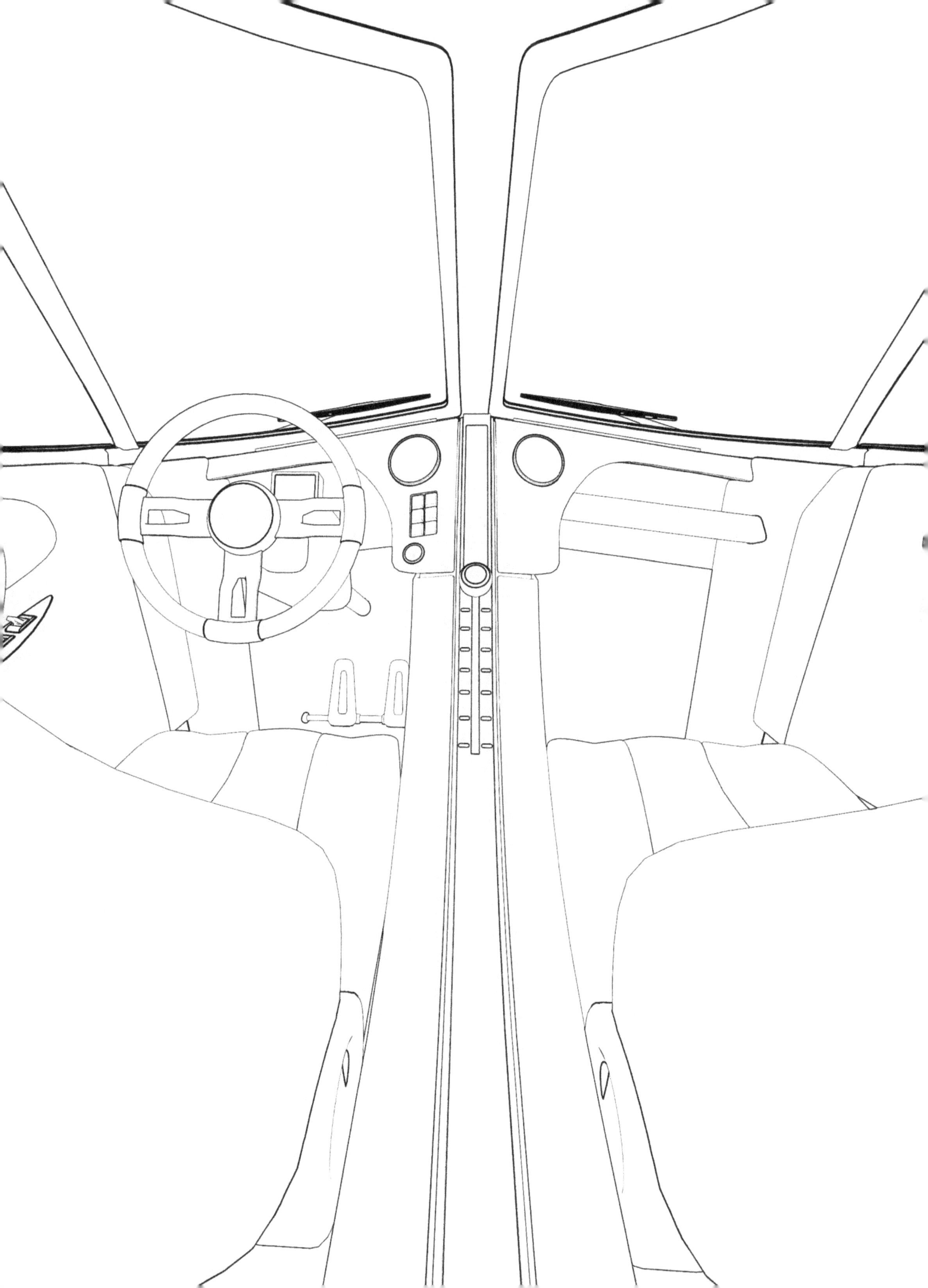

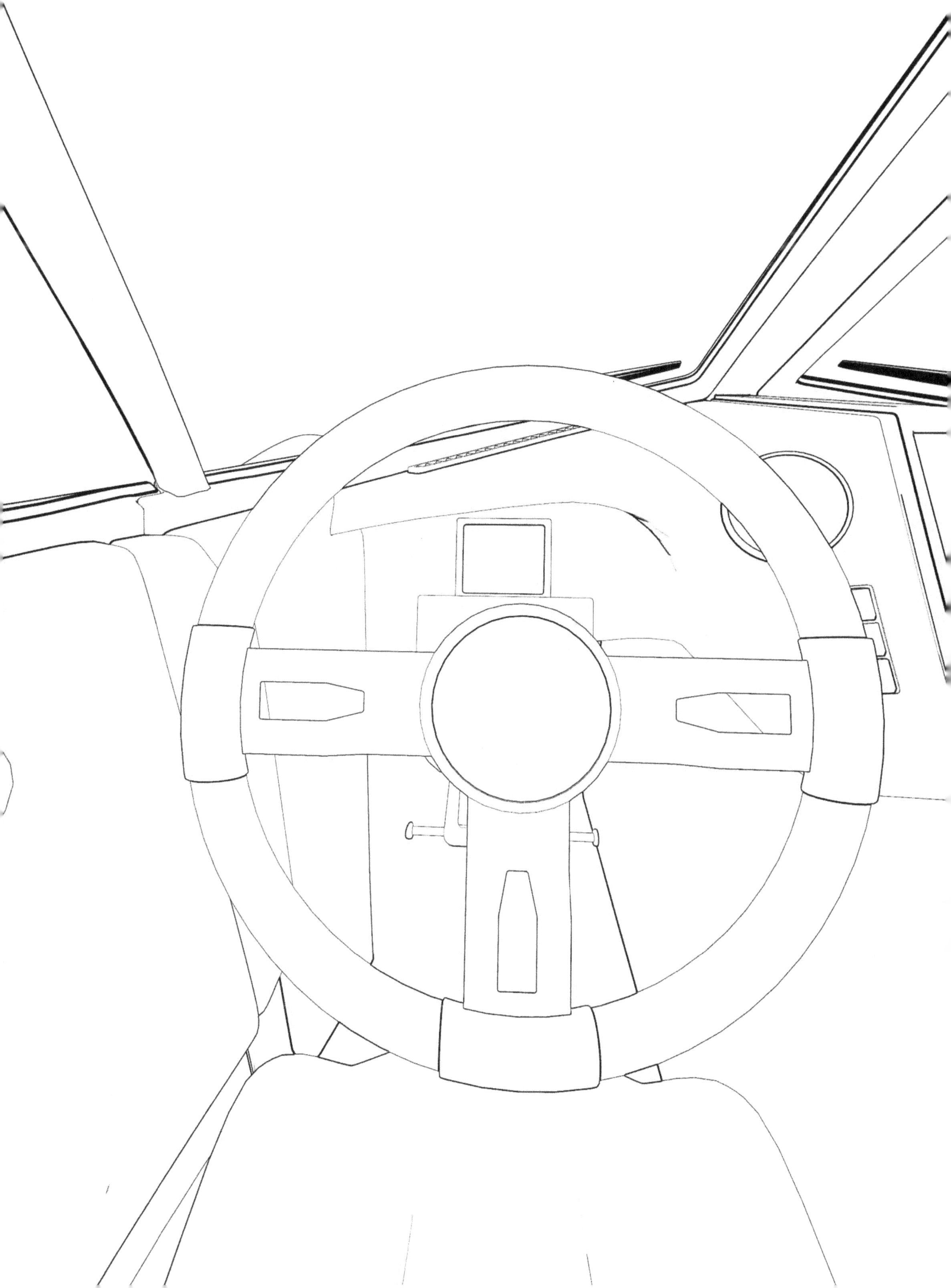

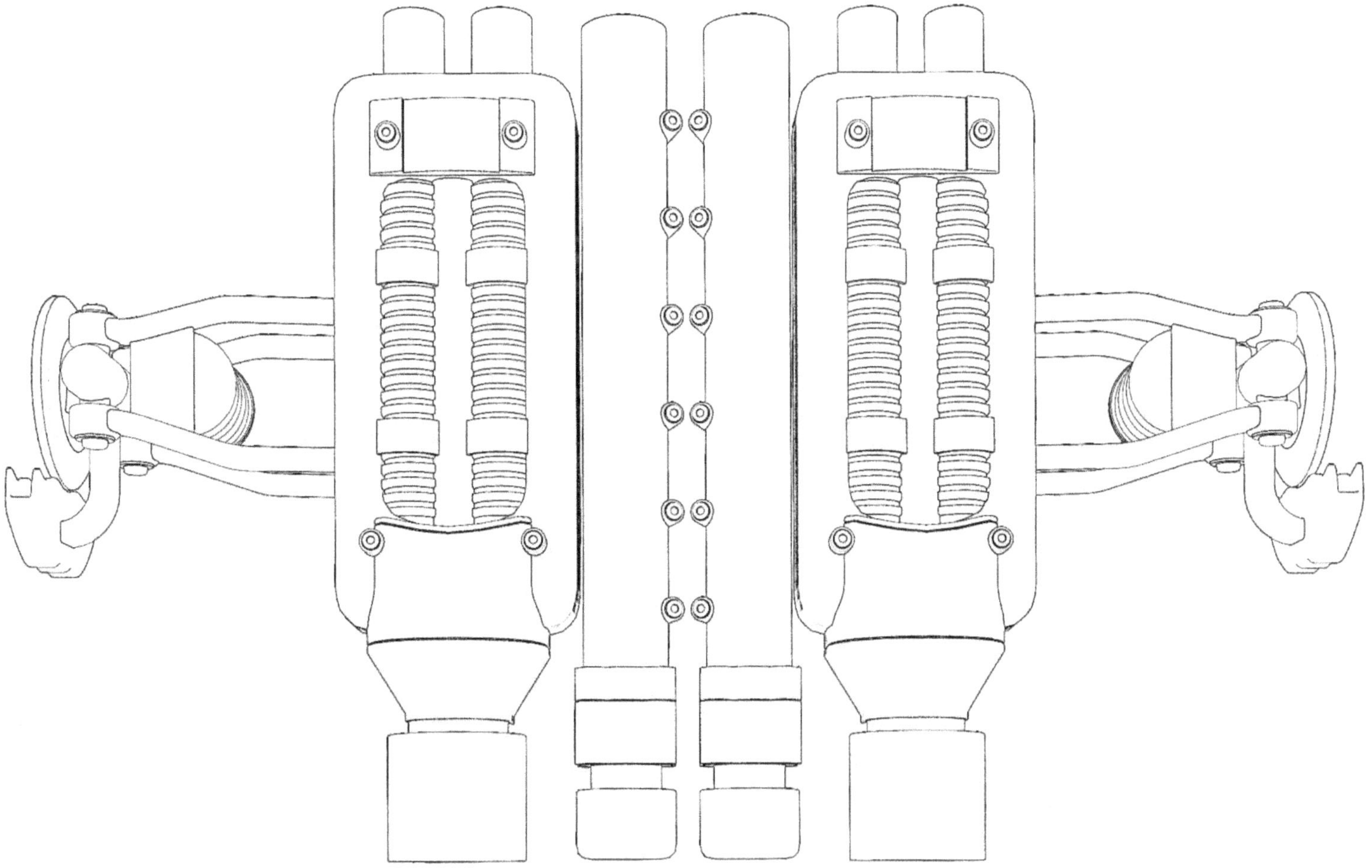

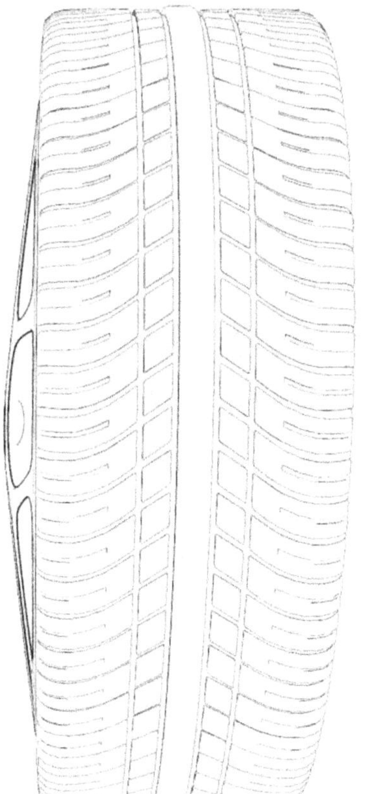

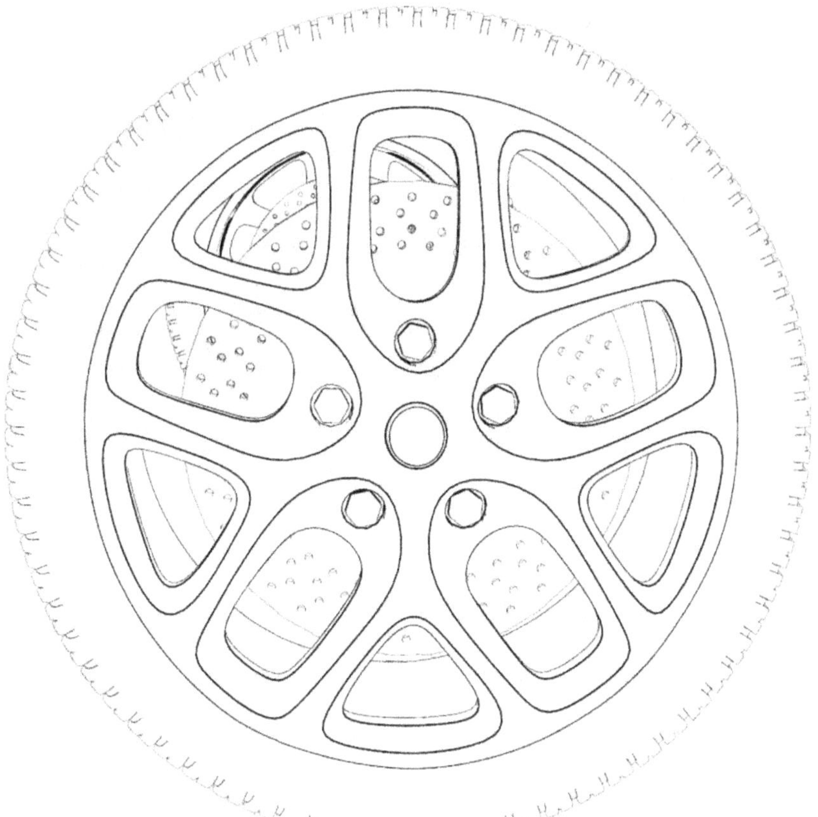

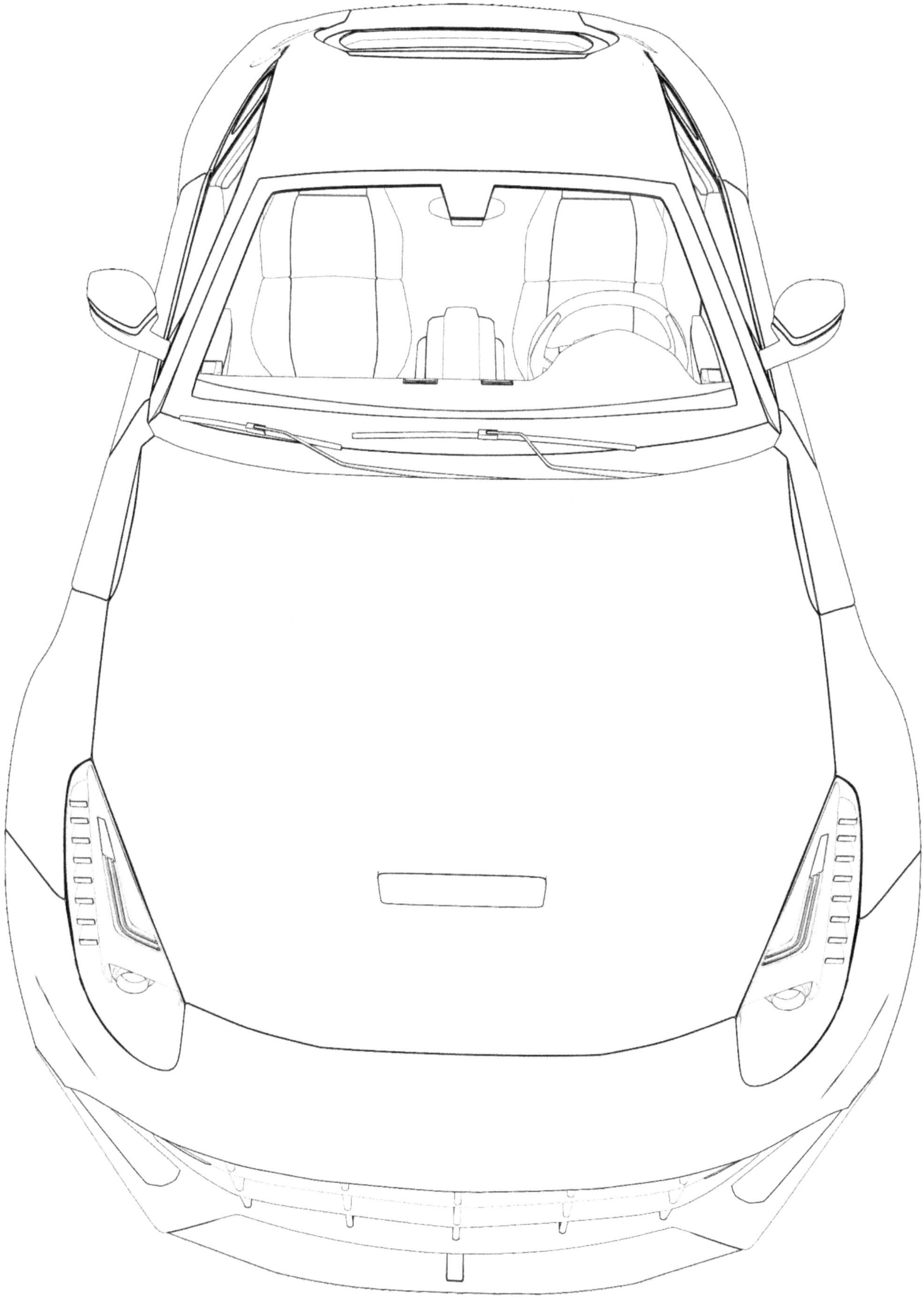

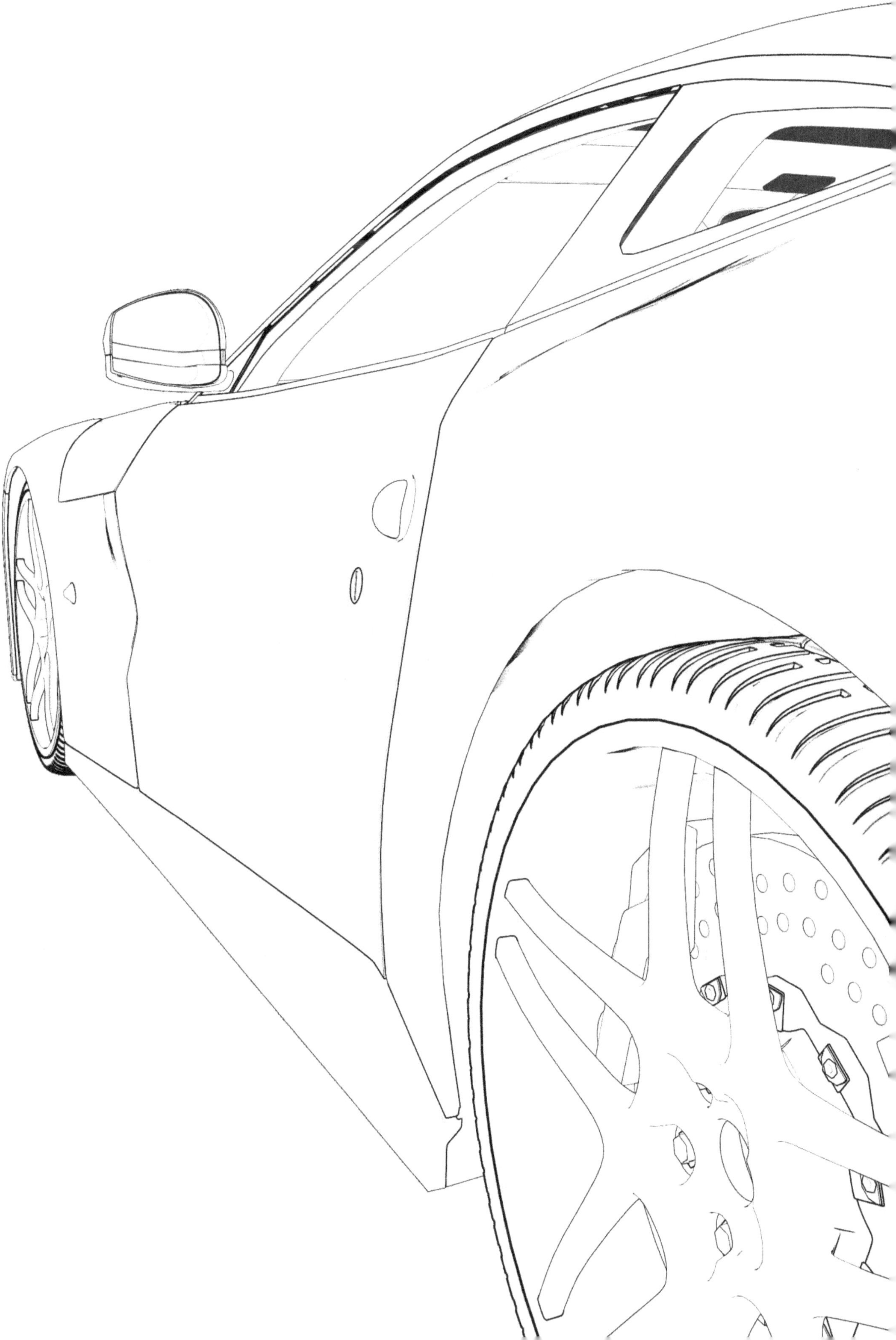

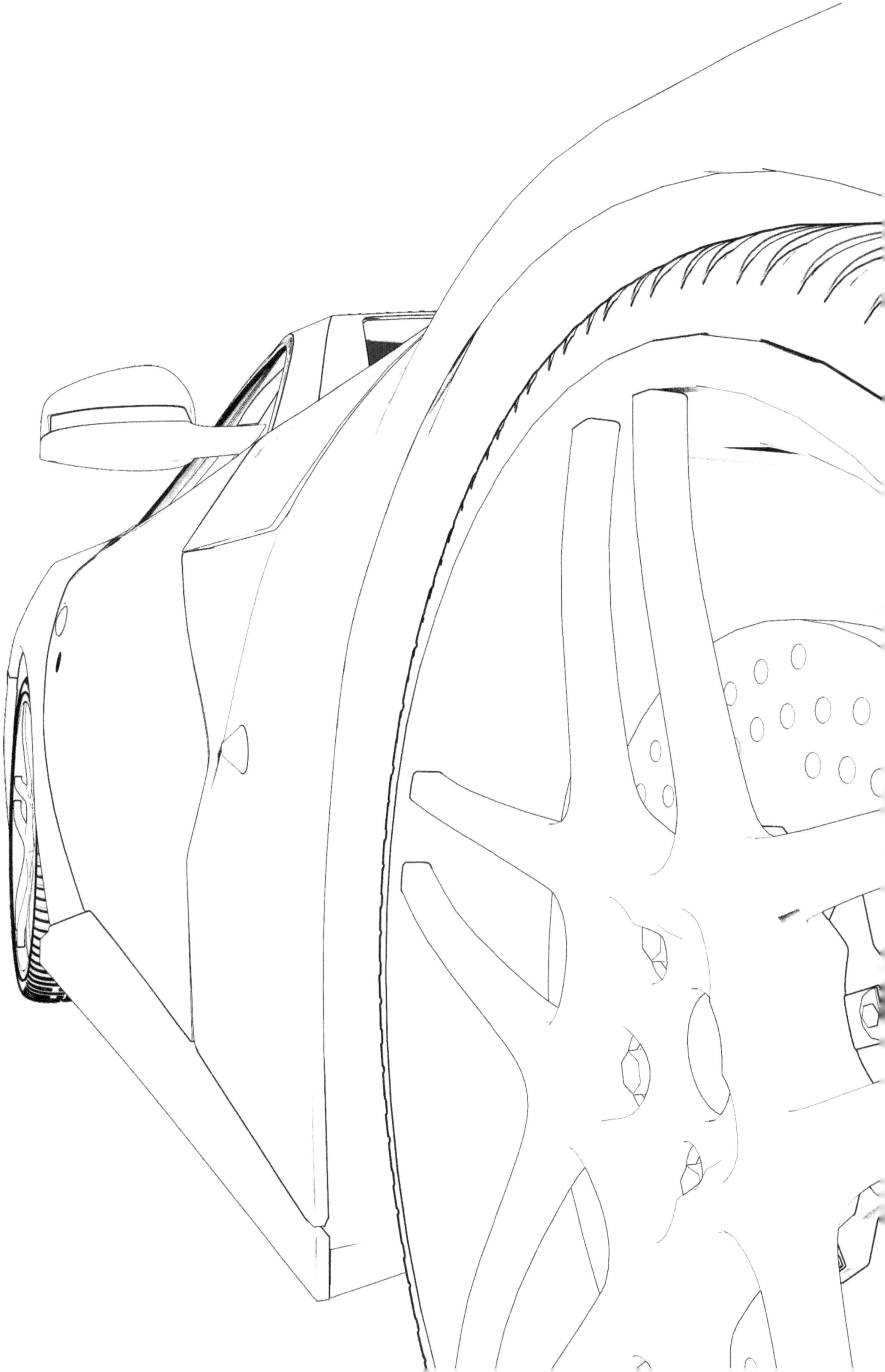

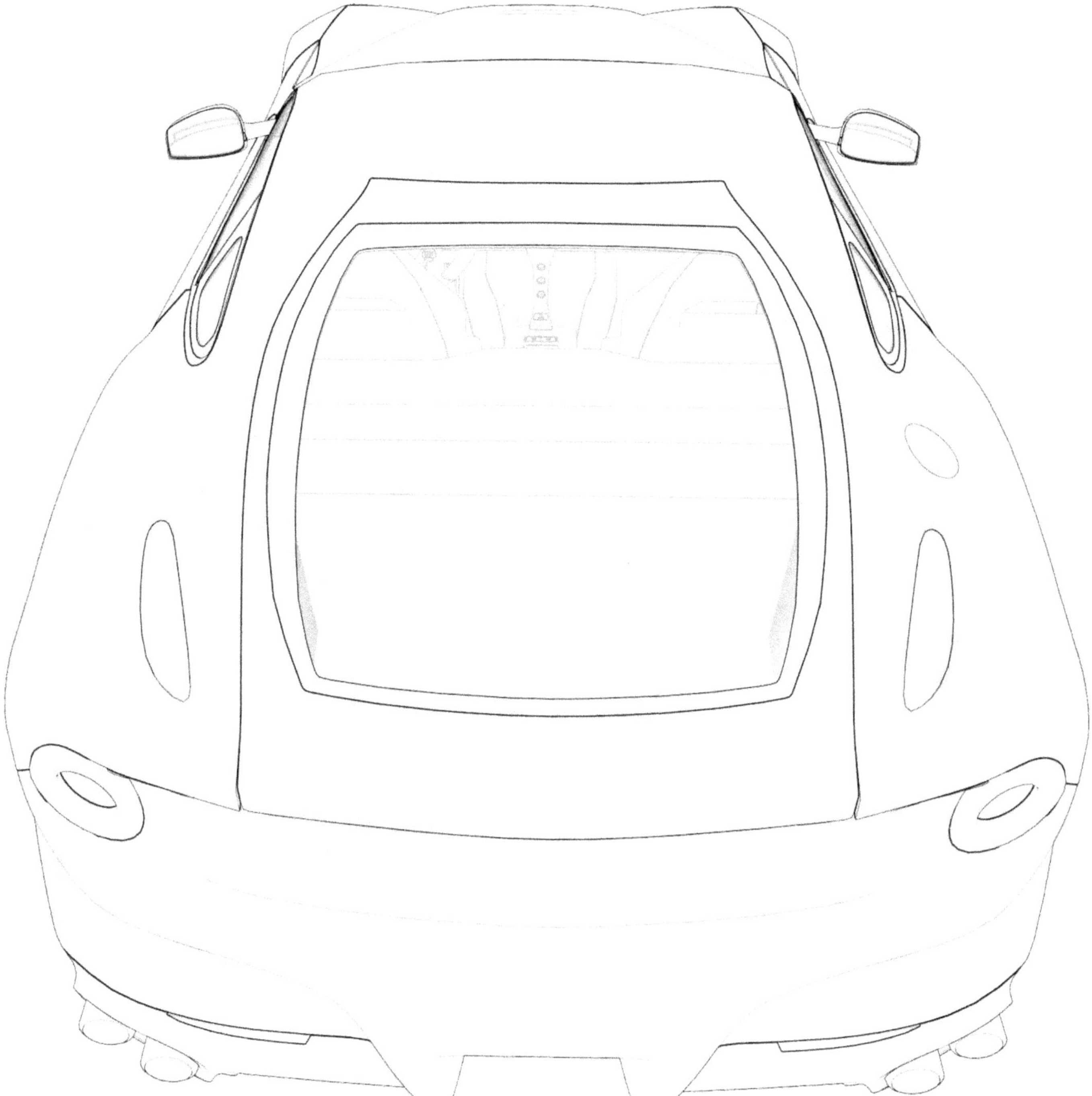

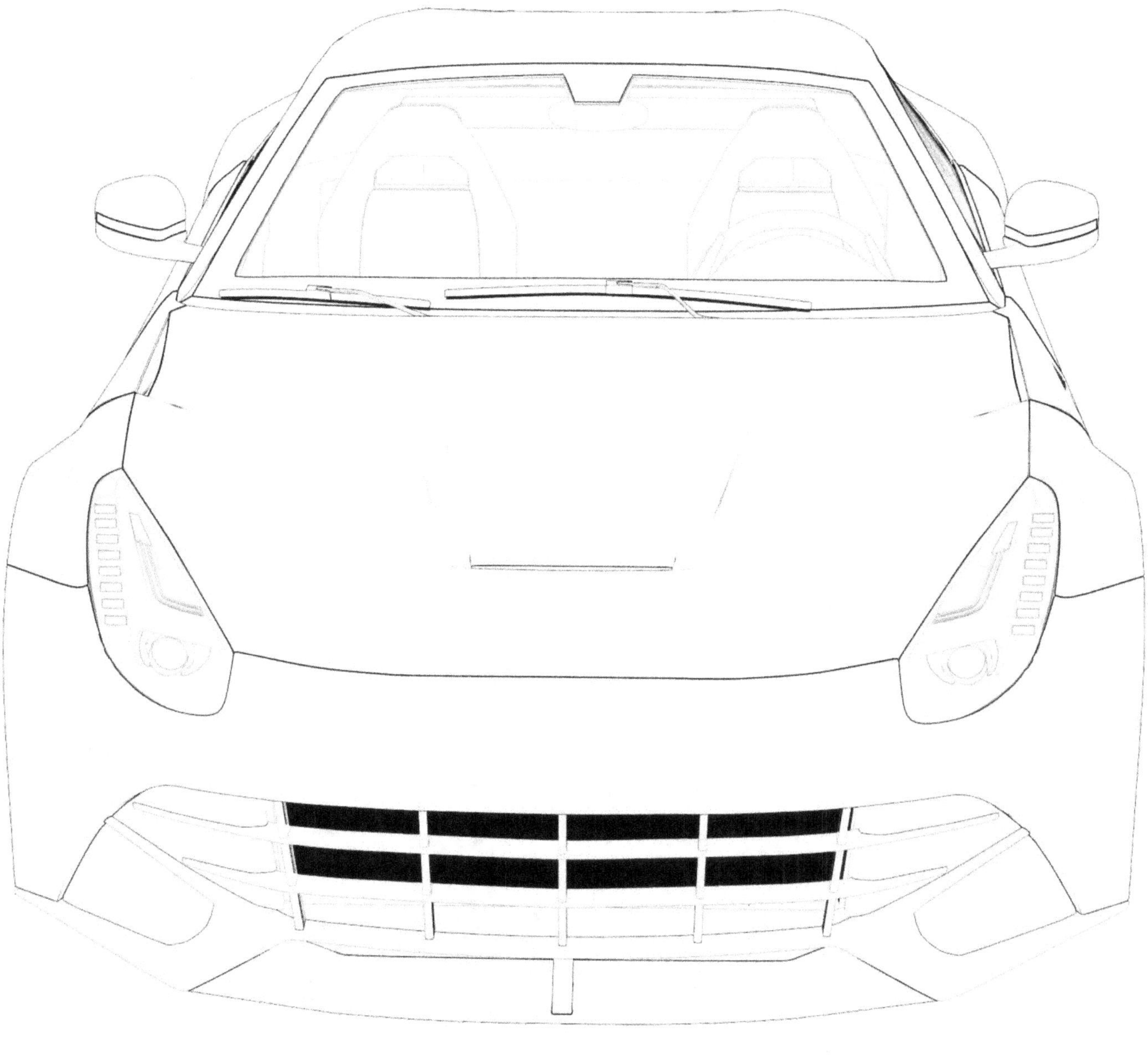

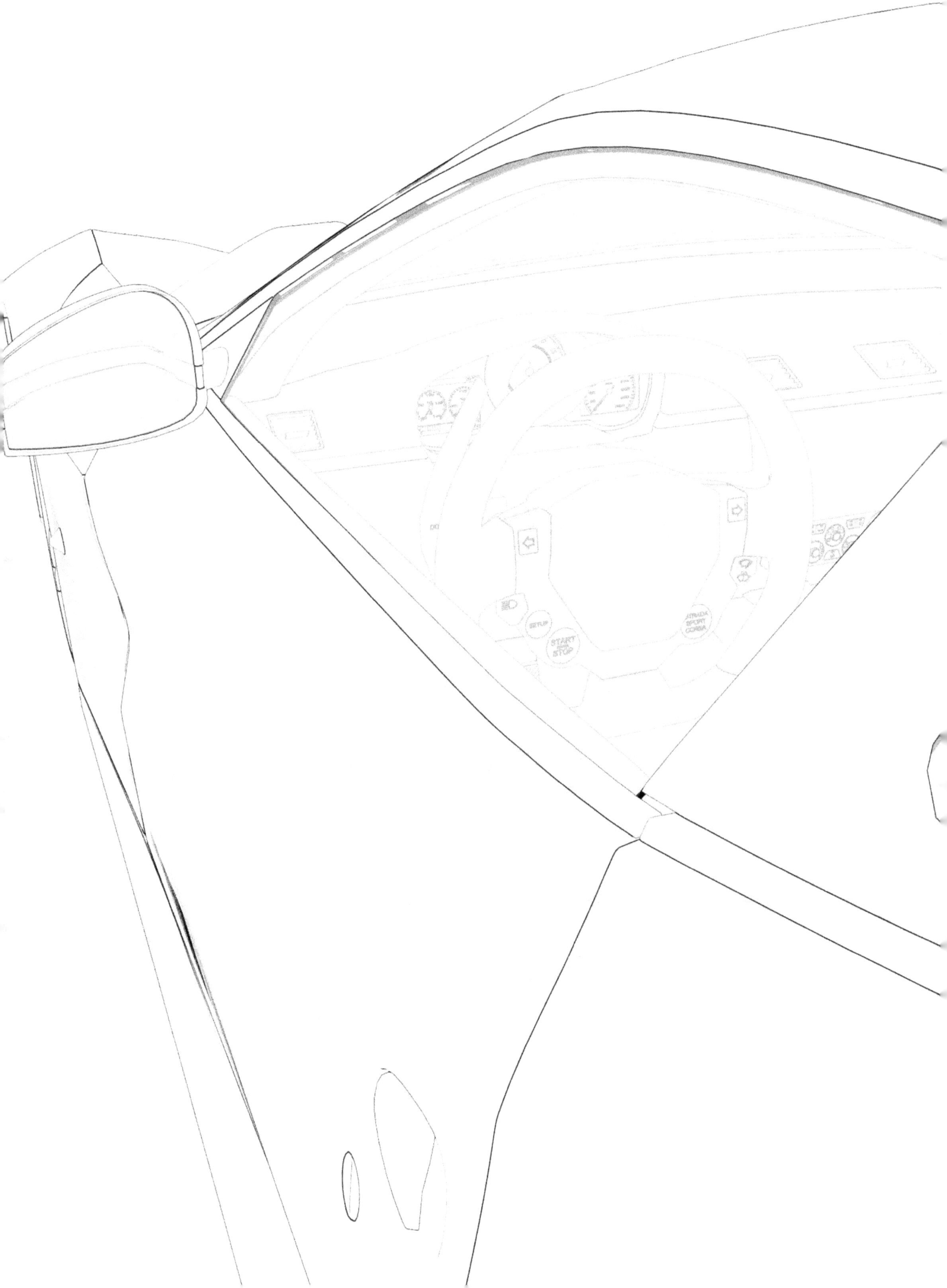
SETUP
START
STOP
STRADA
SPORT
CORSA

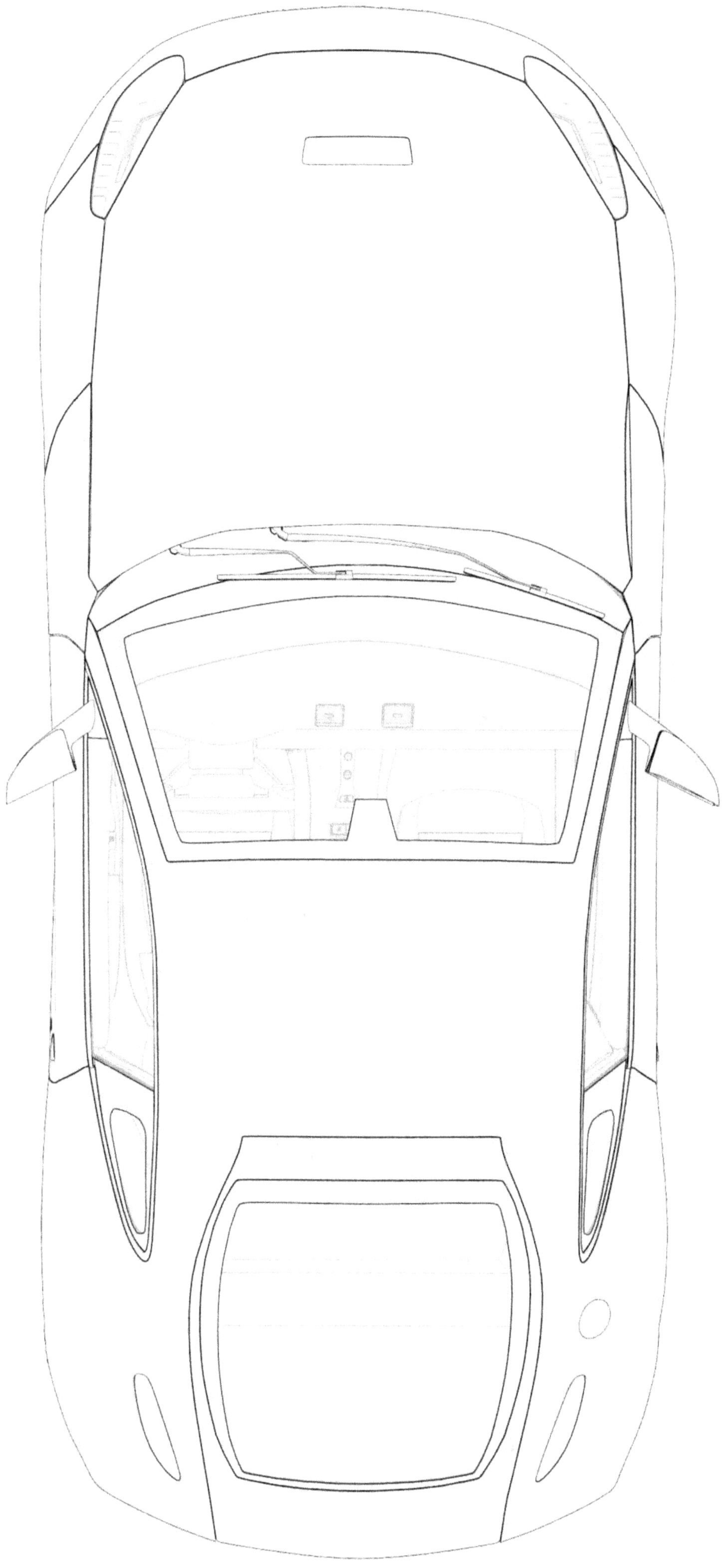

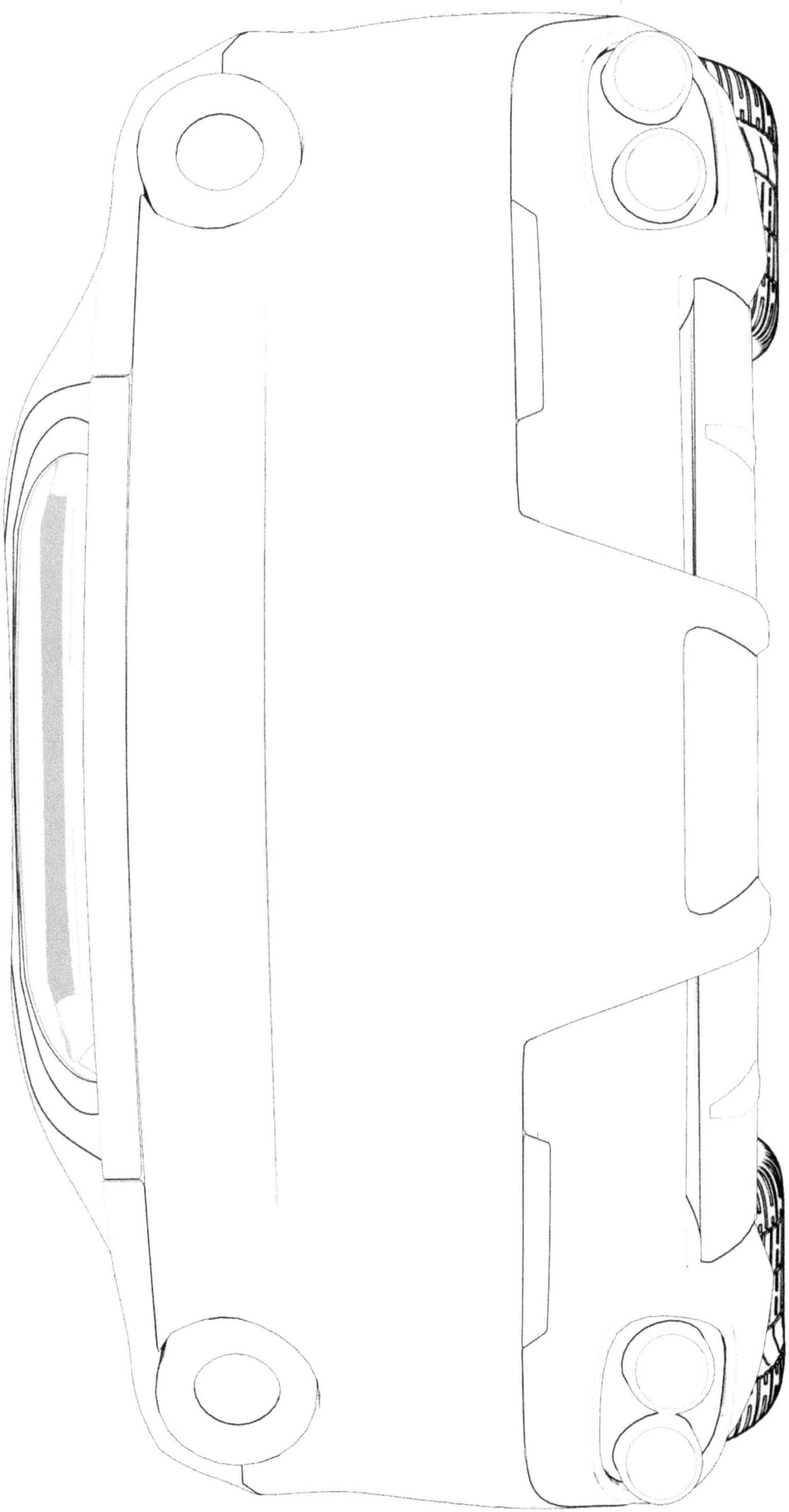

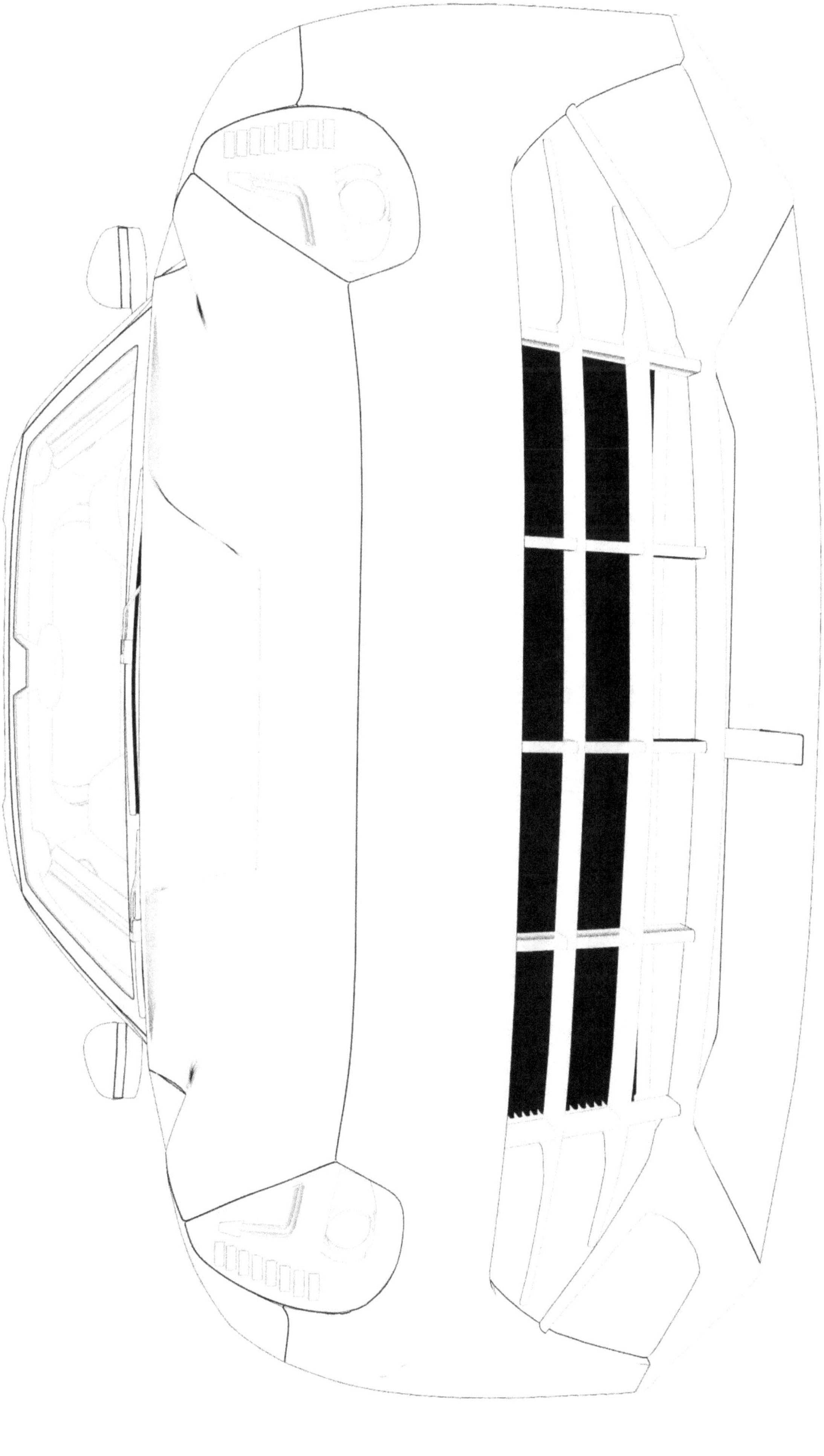

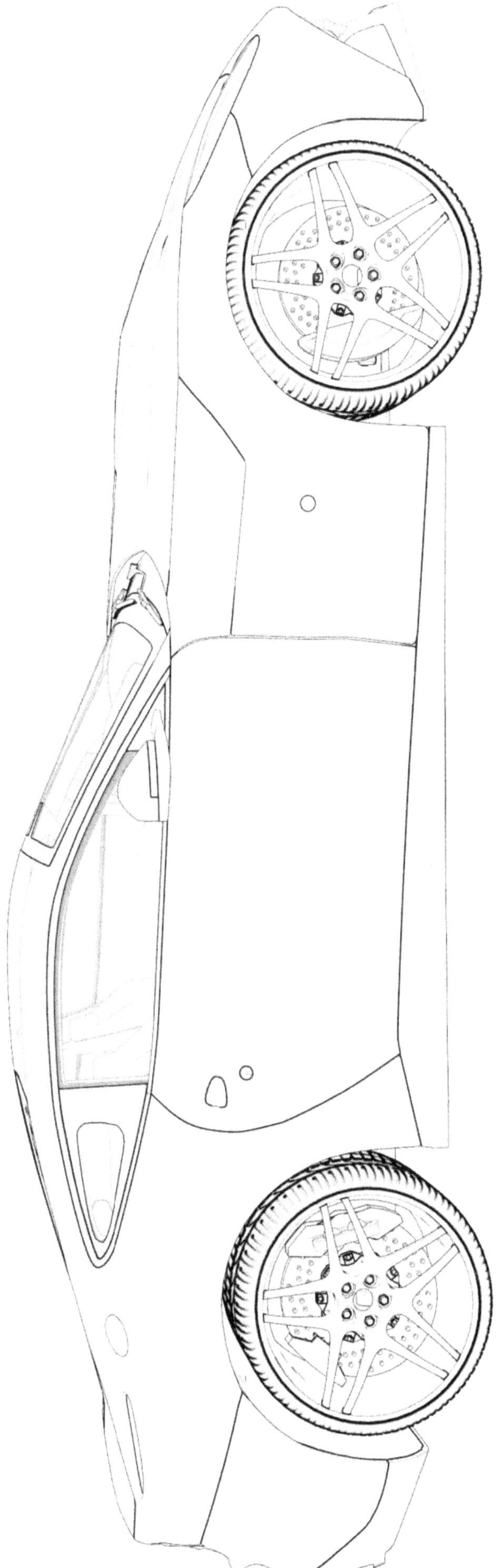

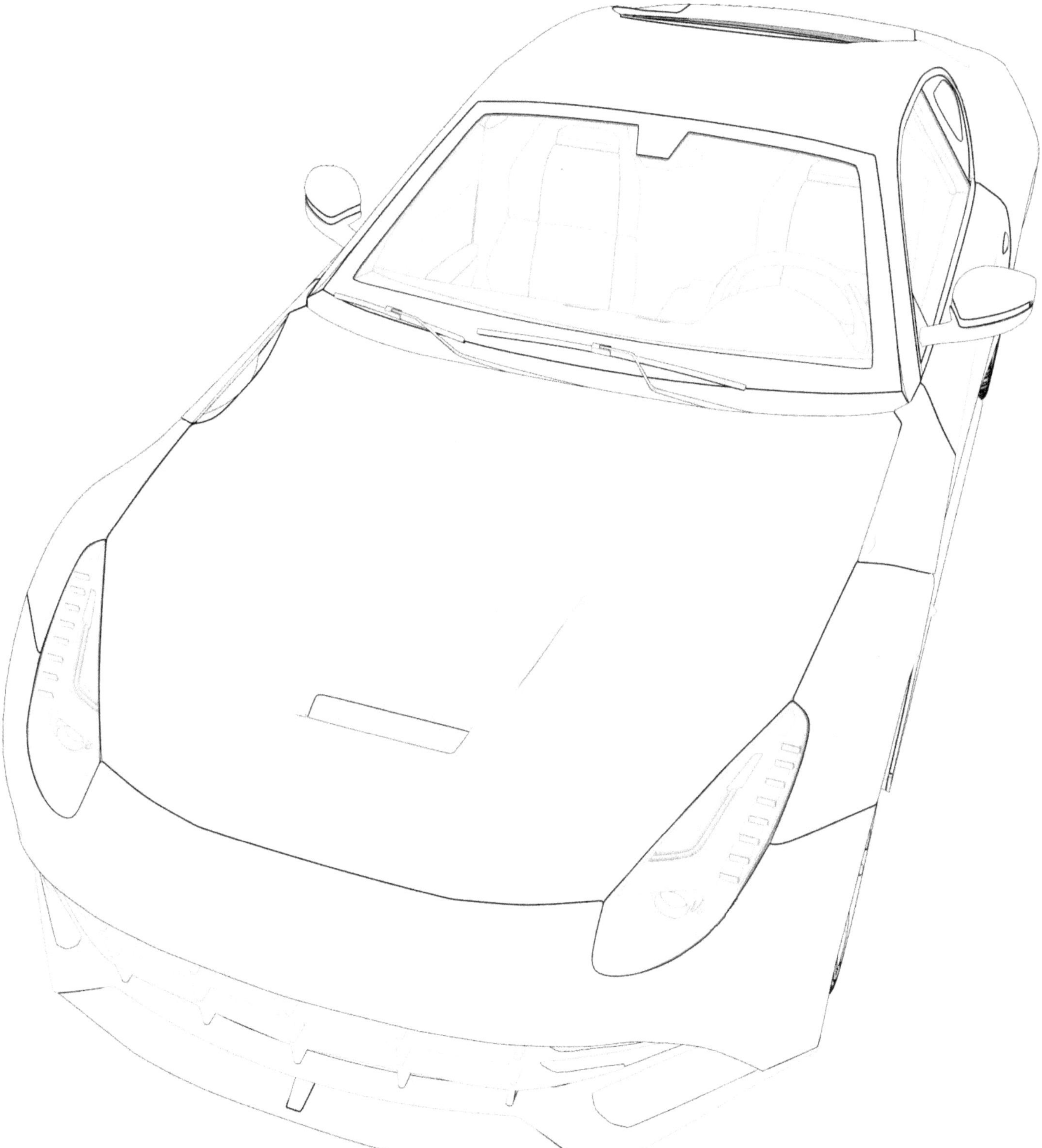

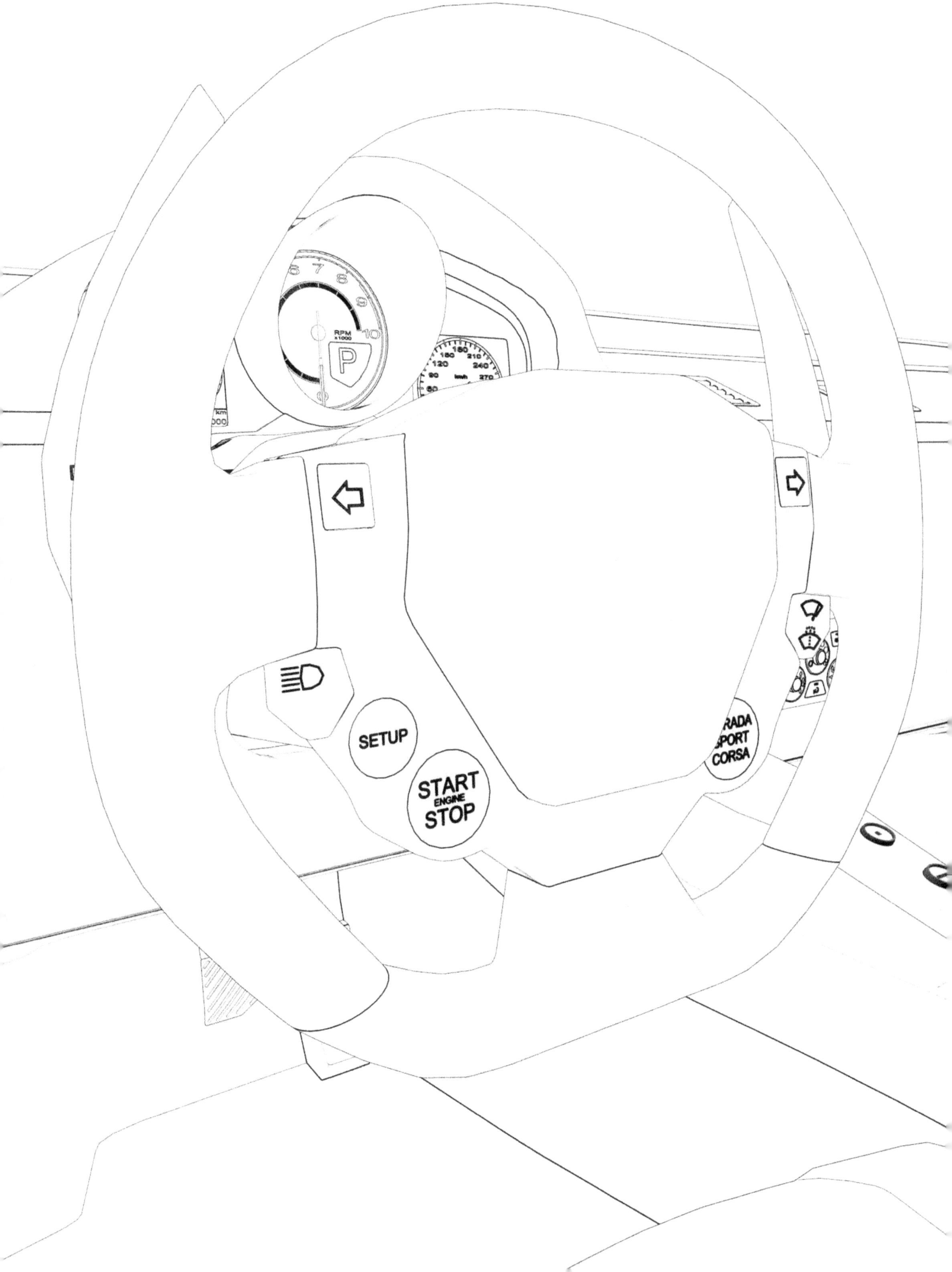
RPM
x1000
P
SETUP
START
ENGINE
STOP
CORSA

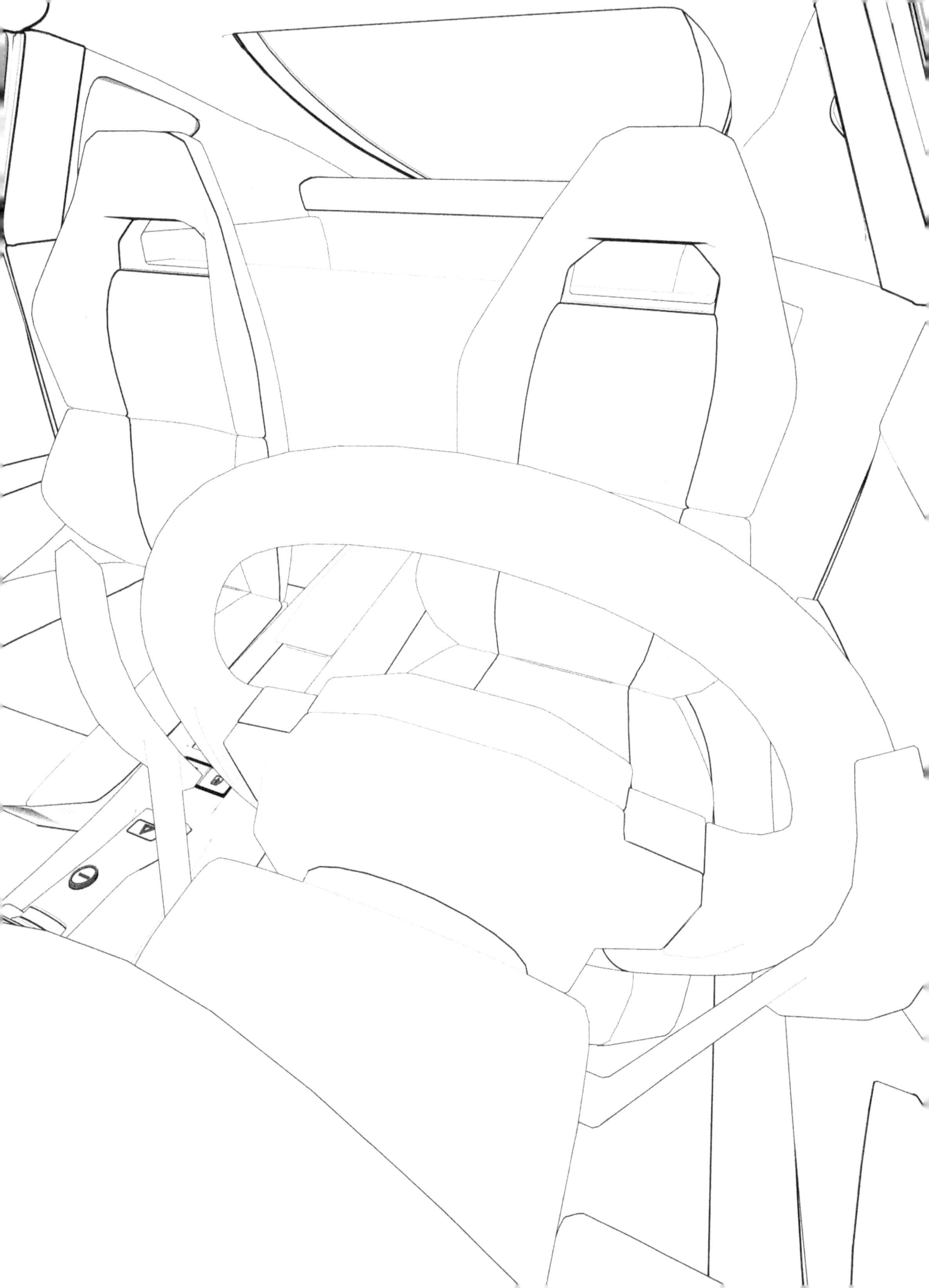

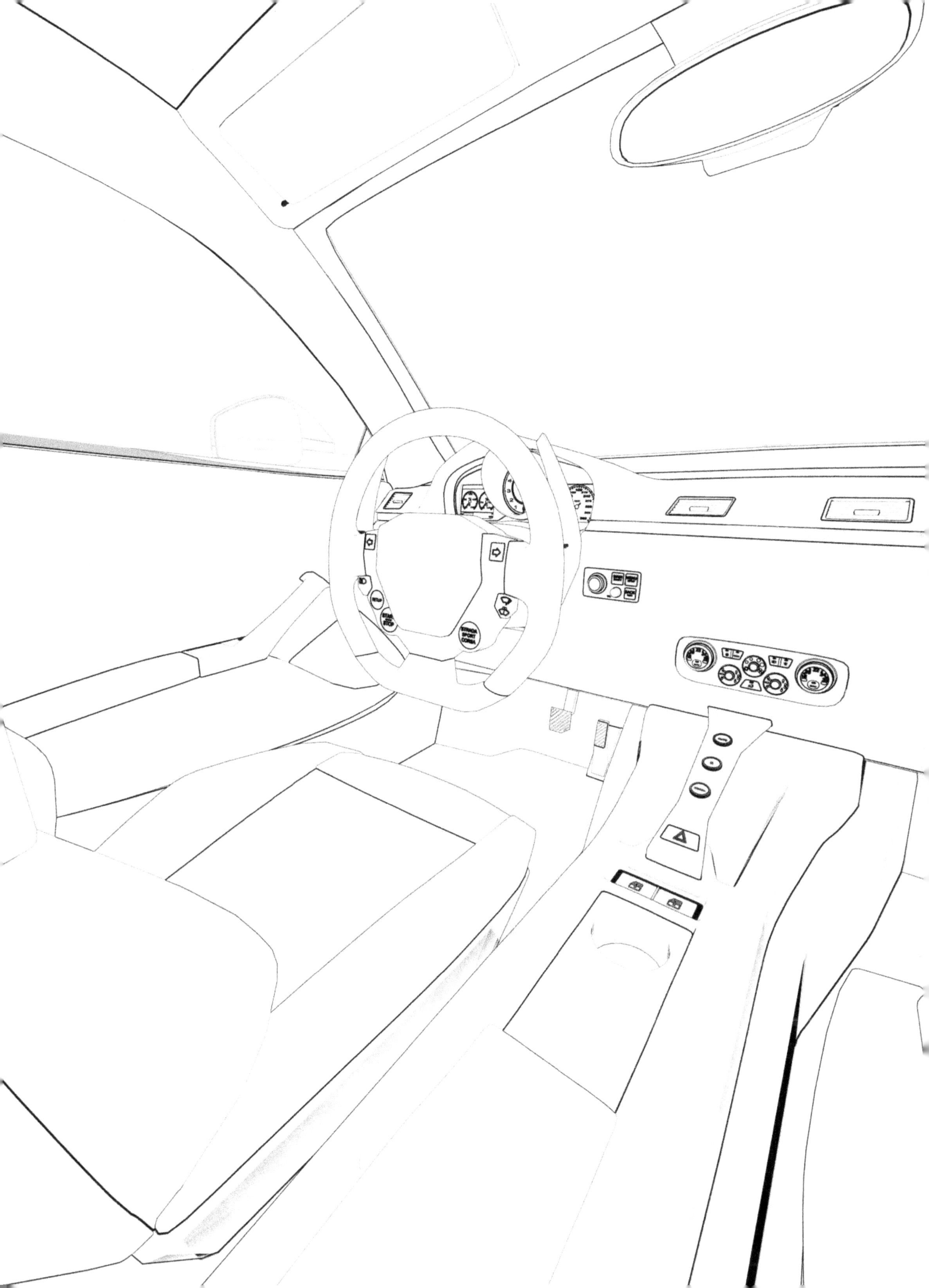
STRADA
SPORT
CORSA

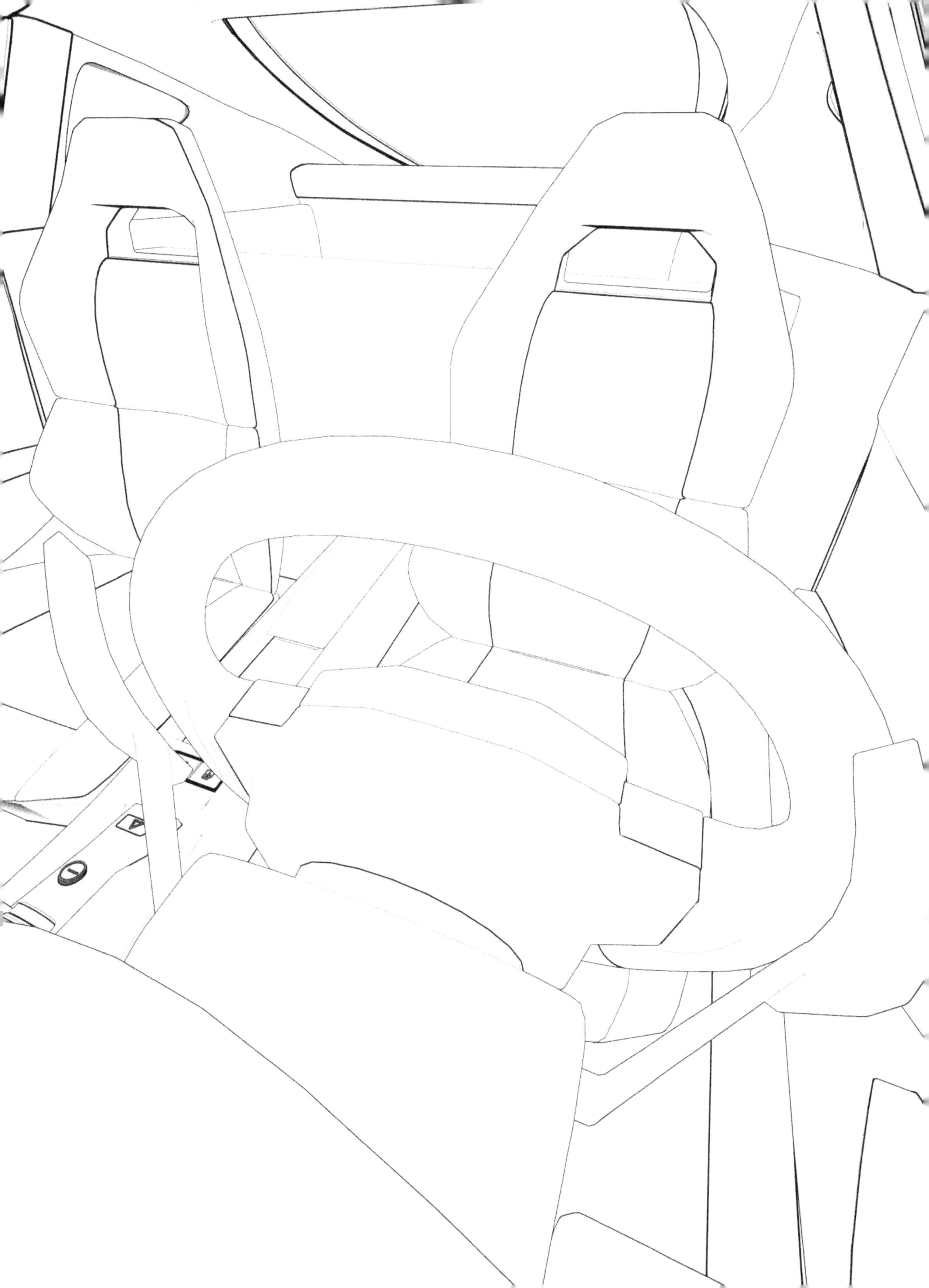

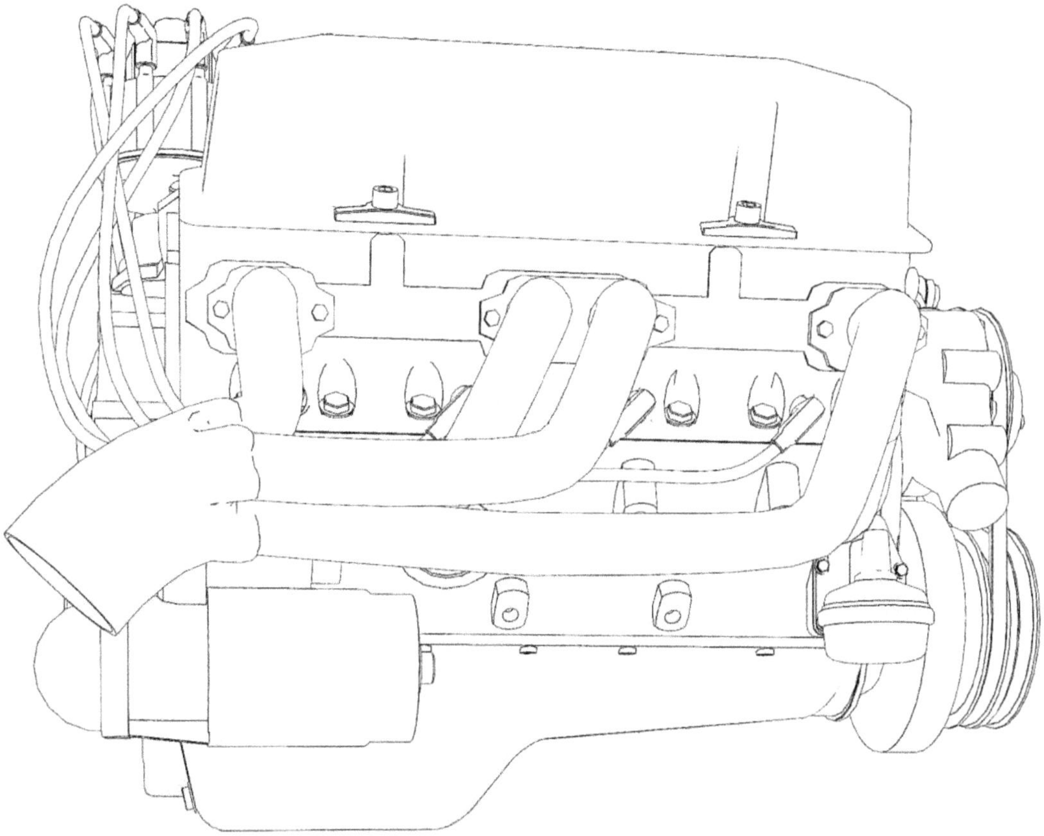

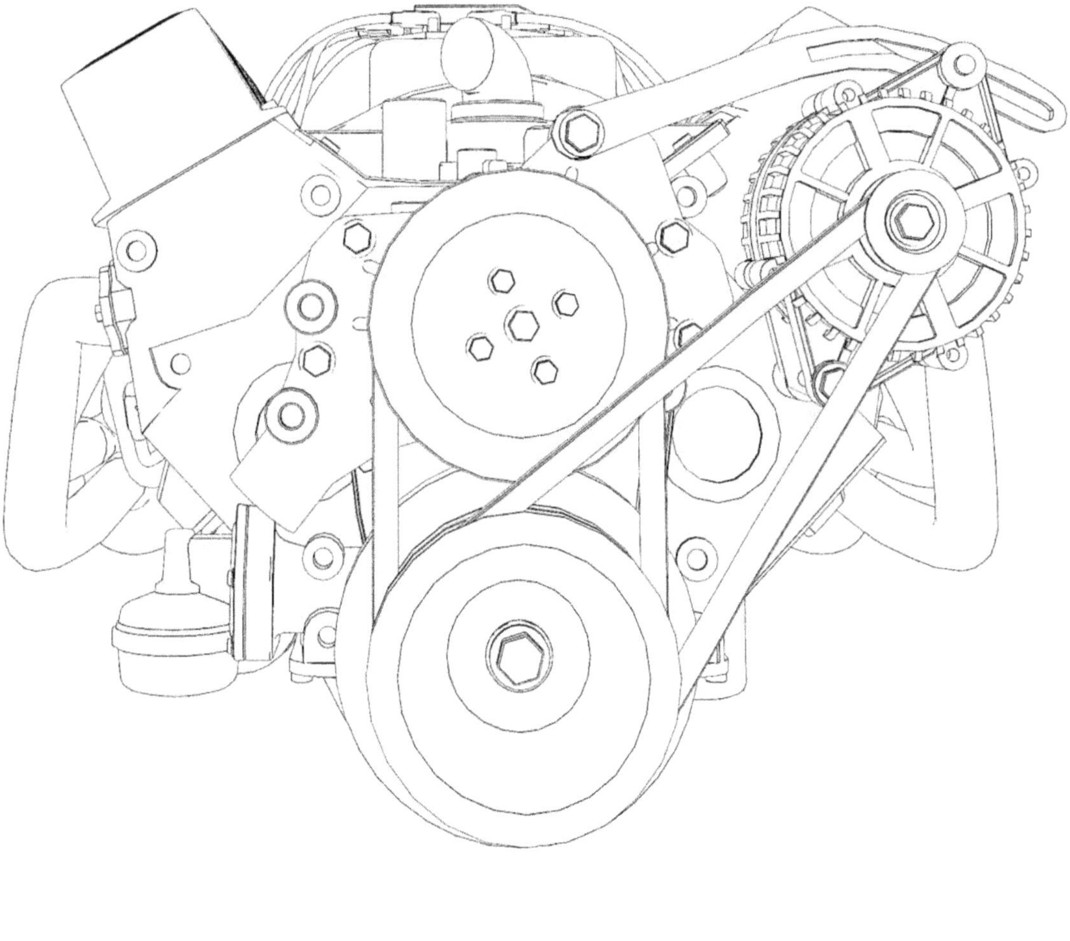

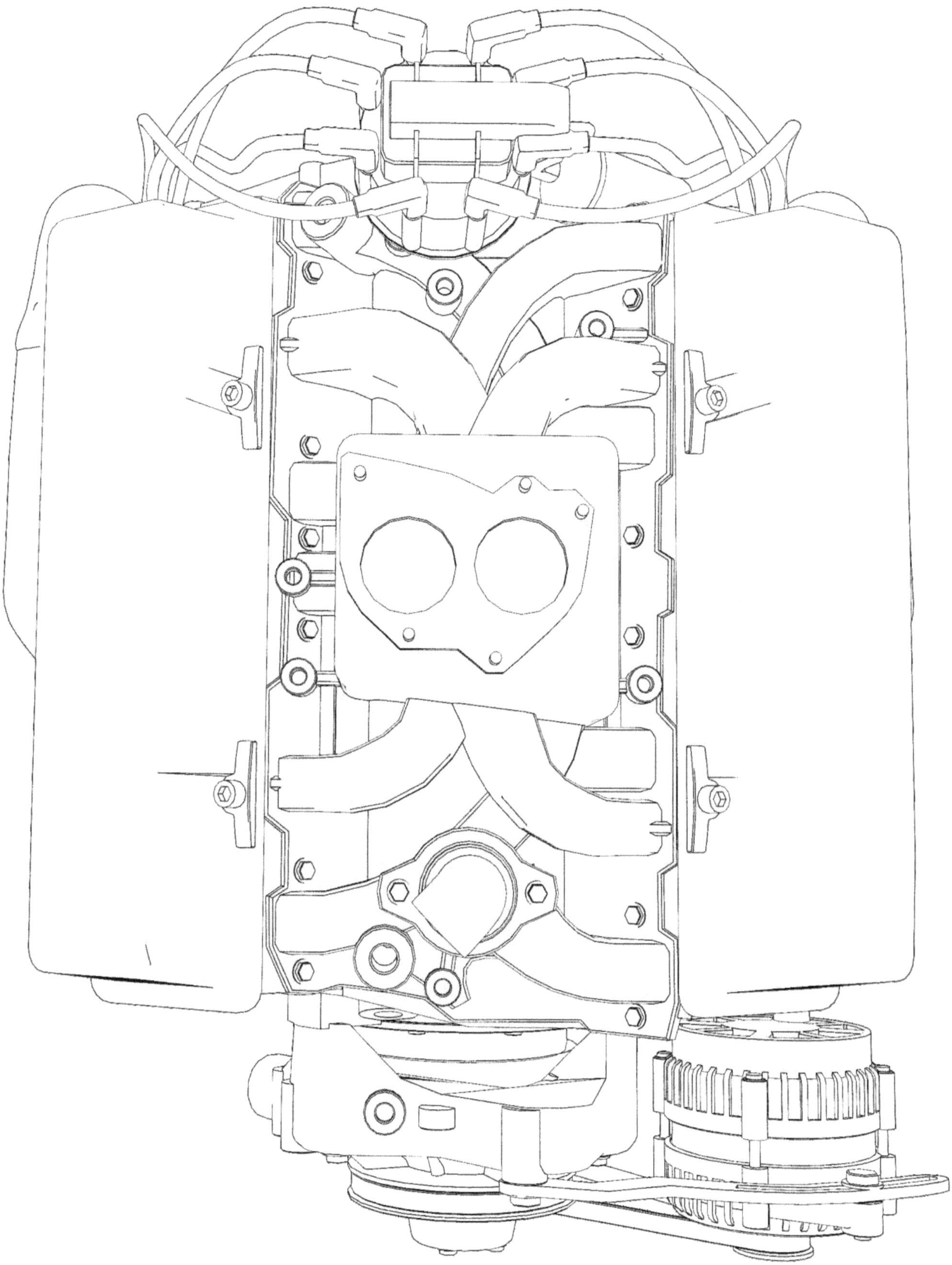

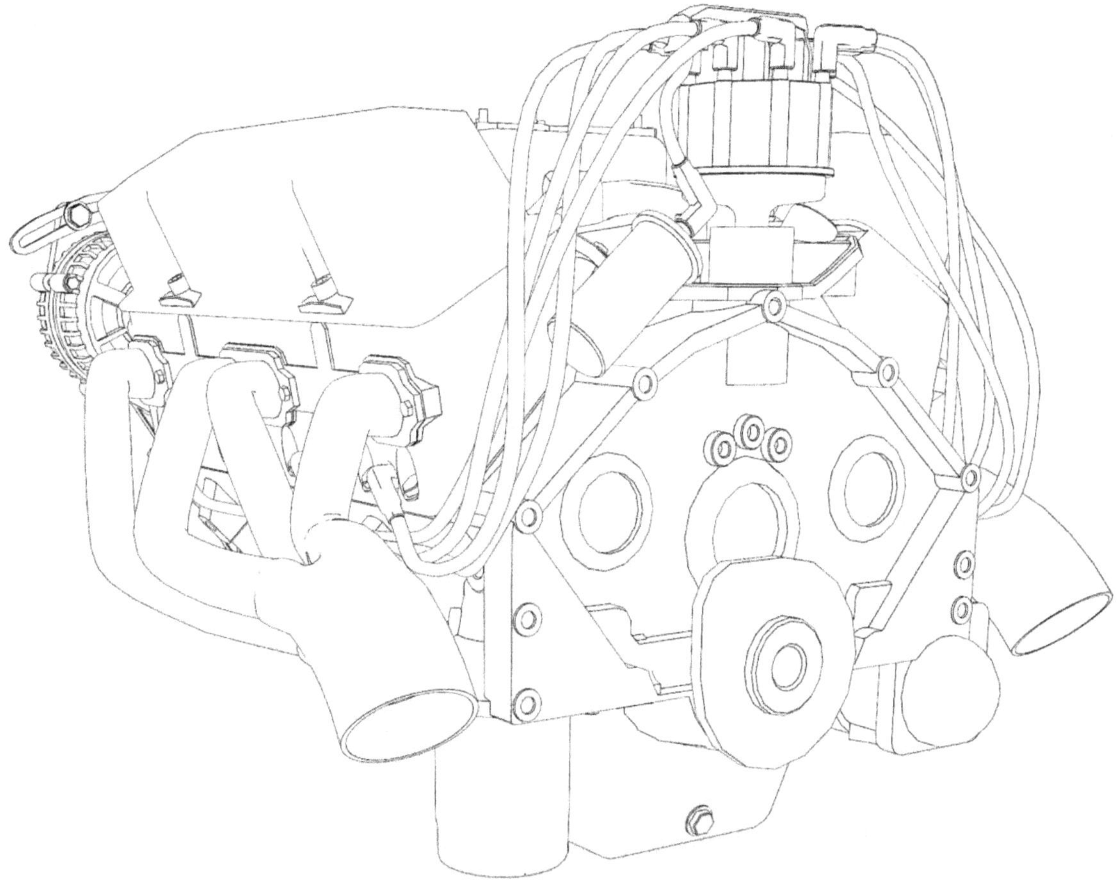

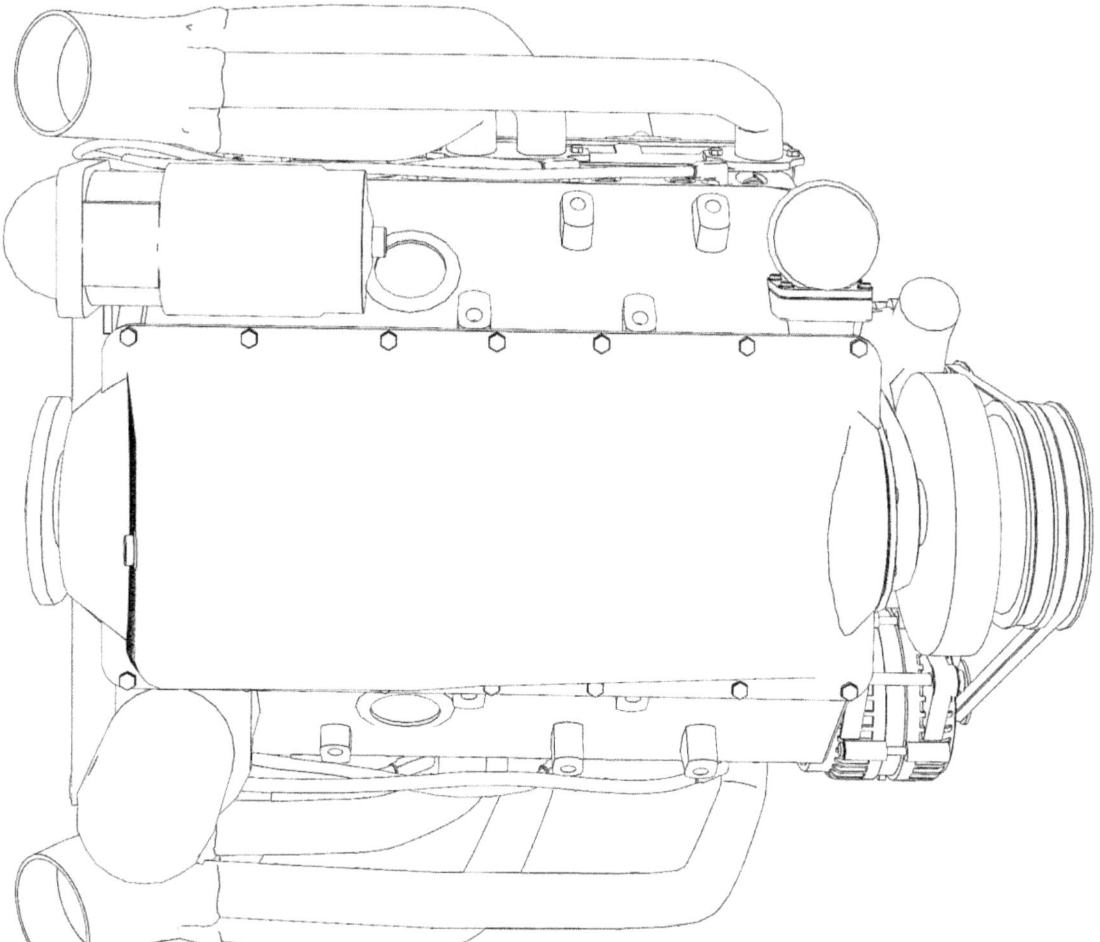

www.ingramcontent.com/pod-product-compliance
Lightning Source LLC
Chambersburg PA
CBHW081607220526
45468CB00010B/2803